ARE YOU HEARING HIM?

ARE YOU HEARING HIM?

The Path

to our

Fourth

Awakening

Donnel McLean

WinePressPublishing
Great Books, Defined.

WinePress Publishing (PO Box 428, Enumclaw, WA 98022) functions only as book publisher. As such, the ultimate design, content, editorial accuracy, and views expressed or implied in this work are those of the author.

All Scripture references, unless otherwise indicated, are taken from the *King James Version*. Authorized King James Version.

Scripture references marked NIV are taken from the *Holy Bible, New International Version*®, *NIV*®. Copyright © 1973, 1978, 1984, 2010 by Biblica, Inc.™ Used by permission of Zondervan. All rights reserved worldwide. www.zondervan.com

Scripture references marked TLB are taken from *The Living Bible*, © 1971 owned by assignment by Illinois Regional Bank N.A. (as trustee). Used by permission of Tyndale House Publishers, Inc., Wheaton, Illinois 60189. All rights reserved.

Scripture reference marked TNIV is taken from the *Holy Bible, Today's New International Version*®. Copyright © 2001, 2005 by Biblica®. Used by permission of Biblica®. All rights reserved worldwide.

ISBN 13: 978-1-4141-2006-5
ISBN 10: 1-4141-2006-0
Library of Congress Catalog Card Number: 2010942710

CONTENTS

Author's Note vii

1. Our Fourth Awakening—Soon? 1
2. Oh, Lord, Help Us! 7
3. As in the Days of Noah 13
4. What? Could Ye Not Watch with Me One Hour? . . 19
5. Bind the Strong Man...Now!. 25
6. Why?. 31
7. Political? Not Really! 35
8. They Are Winning! 41
9. What Are We Doing to Win the Lost? 45
10. Is It Right?. 53
11. Woe to a People Who Offend Their Little Ones . . . 59
12. An Absolute Must! 67
13. Revivalists 73
14. Christian America? 79
15. Only Imagine. 85

16. The Name Above All Names: Jesus! 91
17. A Prayer for America. 99
18. Last Chance, America? 105

Appendix: Voting, an Important Duty 111

Endnotes 115

AUTHOR'S NOTE

TODAY, NATIONWIDE, WE are facing many crises. The dark clouds looming on the horizon spell disaster! In direct response, the Church of Jesus Christ needs to pay attention to what is happening and take courageous action to become His instrument in righting each issue and restoring America to its Christian roots. This book is a passionate call to churches all across America to hear and obey God's clearly spelled out command to unite in days of prayer and fasting—for it is only then that the outpouring will happen.

Chapter 1

OUR FOURTH
AWAKENING — SOON?

WHEN WE SERIOUSLY consider the unparalleled levels of corruption and wickedness that exist in our nation today, we see our righteous God has no choice but to pour out His wrath *if we don't respond to His passionate calls to fasting in prayer* (see Joel 2). We must understand that there comes a time when a nation's cup of iniquity is full and the Almighty has to judge and, at times, destroy a people. This question begs an answer. Are we there…or almost there?

Do you remember why God, in His omniscience, foretold the future destruction of the nations living in Canaan, the Promised Land? Have you ever seriously considered His prophecy to Abraham in Genesis 15? *"Know of a surety that thy seed shall be a stranger in a land that is not theirs, and shall serve them; and they shall afflict them four hundred years…but in the fourth generation they shall come hither again: for the iniquity of the Amorites is not yet full*" (vv. 13,16). But it would be. God gave the Caananites another 400 years to repent, but they didn't! This is the lesson: when any peoples' cup of iniquity is full, the Lord has to judge them. This is profoundly serious.

The vital question today in America is whether or not our cup of iniquity is brimful or if it is almost so. Considering the levels of iniquity here in our homeland, we have to acknowledge that it's probably full, and maybe almost overflowing—and we have the Word of God, which the Canaanites didn't have. We're at the danger point. It would seem that the Lord is weighing America.

We all are painfully aware of the appalling levels of corruption in which our beloved homeland is drowning. For example, we're seeing moral actions today that were unthinkable 30–40 years ago! Crime, violence, and drugs are at epidemic levels here in America. Our rate of incarceration is over seven times higher than most other countries. The phenomenal increase in knowledge, as was predicted by the prophet Daniel 2,500 years ago (see Dan. 12:4), has resulted in unparalleled new levels of evil. Consider the influences of TV, the Internet, the movie industry, and many others—all of which have resulted in unbelievable depths of sexual perversion and addictions. When statistics say that thirty percent of ministers are hooked on pornography, we should be aghast—yes, even sick at heart—wondering just what percentage of the nation is enmeshed in sexual perversion. This includes our precious children.

Remember this: when a nation goes totally berserk morally, it is in its final stages. The end is near! Let's not forget what Alexander Tyler, a Scottish history professor, declared about every previous civilization: *the final stage has always been a total moral collapse, sexual perversion unlimited!* This should make us shudder. Tragically, America is there today...now. It grieves me to have to say this, but it is imperative that we be totally honest about it.

So, sadly (or, better said, terrifyingly), it appears we have reached that level of corruption. It must be so, when our President's appointee for the head of the U.S. Department of Education is Kevin Jennings, founder of the Gay Lesbian and Straight Education Network. Without a doubt, when we are unabashedly teaching our children such vile behavior, it is a sign that America has hit bottom. Truly, we are on the fast track, heading for divine wrath—unless, that is, we repent and go to our knees in the profoundest repentance and concern.

Our nation's virtual worship of sex has resulted in the never-ending murder of millions of precious babies. Multiple other evils also plague us: sexual diseases, greed, divorce, murder, and of course, the rejection of God's Word and Jesus Christ, the Savior. I could go on and on, but that's not my focus here. Rather, I want to declare the facts about where America is today and point out that we are in grave danger of receiving God's divine wrath.

This is a very, very strong warning. *It's a passionate call to God's people...to the Church in America!* It's not a time to throw up our hands in despair. Church, we need—desperately need—to be absolutely appalled and filled with a holy fear of the looming divine wrath. We need to be moved to action, to go to our knees, weep, and travail in agonizing intercession for God to move...*to send our fourth awakening.*

Dare I repeat it? This is not a time to throw our hands up in despair. Nor is it a time to give up. Never! *It is a time for us to stand up, to speak up, to repent of our failure to be the salt in our society, and to stop the escalating spiritual decay.* It's time for us to expose boldly and unceasingly the corruption with the truth—God's Word! As the Church of Jesus Christ, we must boldly proclaim it, warning people to repent and cry out to God for mercy. There is a hell. Jesus Christ alone can save us. Oh, let's shout it! It's time to awaken to the seriousness of the hour and to thank God the judgment we deserve has not yet been poured out upon us.

Our God never wants to punish or destroy a people. He longs, rather, to forgive, to bless, and to have millions experience more and more of His love and blessings. Our merciful God yearns passionately for a nationwide stirring of His people who will take the lead—this month, this year, *now*—in true repentance and cry out for mercy. Yes, we need another awakening.

Soak in the awesome message found in the book of Judges. It's the sad story of Israel, God's people, who for 400 years kept falling into the sins of the surrounding nations. This is a vivid portrayal of humankind—and, yes, of us in America today. But, most of all, it is a glorious portrayal of the Almighty's forgiving heart. Every time Israel repented and cried out in abject repentance, God sent deliverers and rescued His people. The message? God never wants to judge or destroy us. He passionately longs for us to repent and seek His forgiveness so that He can pour out His unlimited blessings *and raise up powerfully anointed revivalists to bring another awakening.* Do we really get it? Oh, that the Church would grasp this concept and unite to seek His face right now—for America.

Here is some good news. In 1910, during the Azusa Street Revival that swept around the world, it was prophesied there would be a greater outpouring of God's Spirit in 100 years. Well, that time is now. So get excited. Take action. Beginning now—today, this week—let's heed God's passionate pleas from the book of Joel that no one can possibly misunderstand. Don't you hear Him? *God Himself is beseeching churches all across our city, our state, and our nation to go to our knees as one body.* Let's obey Him. It's absolutely essential we understand the promised next awakening will not—cannot—happen without our travailing in prayer. For this reason, it is of utmost importance that you and I, fellow Christians, come to grips with the necessity of our weeping for the lost.

Now hear our God pleading, *"Therefore also now... turn ye even to me with all your heart, and with fasting, and weeping, and with mourning: And rend your heart, and not your garments, and turn unto the LORD your God....Blow the trumpet in Zion, sanctify a fast, call a solemn assembly: Gather the people....Weep between the porch and the altar, and let them say, Spare thy people, O LORD, and give not thine heritage to reproach, that the heathen should rule over them: wherefore should they say among the people, Where is their God?...The LORD will answer and...will do great things....And it shall come to pass afterward [when we pray and obey!], that I will pour out my spirit upon all flesh; and your sons and your daughters shall prophesy, your old men shall dream dreams, your young men shall see visions....And I will shew wonders....And it shall come to pass, that whosever shall call on the name of the LORD shall be delivered"* (Joel 2:12–13, 15–17, 19, 21, 28, 30, 32).

Fellow Christian, do you truly, even passionately, yearn for another awakening—to see countless lost souls at the altars of our churches meeting our Lord Jesus? Do you long to see unsaved loved ones, neighbors, and friends at the altars as well? Church, beginning now—today—I beg you to heed His call. Obey His voice! Unite in prayer!

Please let this truth grip your soul: *the eternal destiny of thousands, even millions, hinges on our prayers, dear fellow Christian!* That is profoundly serious. Oh that each one of us would grasp it, for then and only then will it come—our fourth awakening! Our part in this equation is of immeasurable importance. How much do we in the Church yearn for that awakening to the degree that we obey His pleas and travail unceasingly for it? *The coming of this awakening depends on our obedience!*

Chapter 2

OH, LORD, HELP US!

NATIONWIDE, THE CHURCH—our own congregations even—seemingly have little or no burden for prayer and little or no real understanding as to its importance. As a direct result, the majority of our churches seldom (if ever) unite as a body to travail in prayer for our nation's deliverance from its rapid fall. This is in spite of our being aware of the rampant evil in our society and the serious misdirection in which our leaders in Washington D.C. are taking us.

This question cries out for an answer: why is there seemingly little or no concern—at least not enough to move us to action—to pray? How is it possible that in such a dark day the Church does not unite in ever-increasing prayer and cry out for God, pleading for His forgiveness? Could it possibly mean our pastors and Christian leaders do not comprehend the power and urgency of our uniting in prayer? It certainly seems so, doesn't it? Oh, how tragic!

Have you seen a church recently calling for even a day of prayer with fasting? Frankly, I haven't. This is a total mystery to me, because in the New Testament we read how the Early Church powerfully portrayed a praying church. In fact, the very kickoff of the flames of fire from heaven, was its uniting in unceasing prayer for ten days in an upper room. It was then the Spirit fell and countless thousands were swept into the kingdom of God. So, if this is the case, why doesn't the Church today follow suit? Certainly God's methods have not changed. The chief characteristic of that Early Church was prayer—unceasing prayer! How I thank God that there are a few churches that mobilize to fast and pray! But, sadly, I haven't seen any, and this profoundly concerns me.

Back in the 1960s, the Church in America cancelled its weekly, traditional prayer meetings. Oh, how subtly and silently the enemy had struck a killing blow! It is imperative for us to recognize the enemy's tactics. From that time on, the extreme escalation of corruption in this country literally exploded—including the legalizing of abortion on demand. Talk about capitulation to the enemy. We, Christ's followers, have done it big time. We have failed as His Church through our silence and our failing to stop the corruption. Our national sin is immeasurable. What is also wicked is our seeming acceptance of the continued massacre of millions of our nation's precious babies. Church, we are guilty.

We have not united, we have not wept brokenheartedly together, and we have not risen as one voice to demand this practice be stopped *now*. How is it possible that the majority of us seem unconcerned and are not involved? How many of us have ever even prayed about it? How is it even possible that Christians actually have become used to this practice of our nation's sacrificing millions of babies on the altars of immorality? Is that not true? Definitely so. Given this, it is only inevitable that God will hold us responsible. Our cry now—today—must be for action, calling every true follower of our Lord Jesus Christ to get concerned and unite as one voice and persist until victory is won and this carnage has stopped.

We're in a war—to the death—against this encroaching evil, and prayer is our mightiest weapon. Yet we have laid it down. Our enemy is unseen: *"For our struggle is not against flesh and blood, but against the rulers, against the authorities, against the powers of this dark world and against the spiritual forces of evil in the heavenly realms"* (Eph. 6:12, TNIV). Today, there is much evidence that we—God's people, His Church—as a whole do not understand this, let alone act on it. Now that is serious, extremely so, for prayer is our greatest weapon in the battle with our unseen enemy.

Apparently, the majority of today's Christians never have been taught the extreme gravity and importance of prayer. Most believers, it seems, know little about personal devotions and interceding for the lost and for the nation. Nor have they experienced deep personal encounters with the Almighty. Given this fact, it is only logical that most have no real understanding as to the extreme importance and absolute necessity of having personal prayer times and gathering together as a body in our churches and/or homes to pray and weep together for the lost and for the nation.

Tragically, it seems there are even pastors who do not have private devotions where they can encounter the glory of God's sweet presence and travail in prayer for the lost. This is sad, because if these pastors really understood it, they would realize it is *only* when they spend time in the Lord's presence that the anointing will come on their ministries. If our leaders do not understand the importance of prayer, it is only logical their people won't either.

Thank God there are intercessors who are praying and *uniting* in prayer. Hallelujah! Glory to God! No doubt, this is what is keeping us from receiving divine judgment in this day. Yes, thank God for every intercessor—and for every gathering of intercessors as well. Oh, how awesome are the Jesus Houses of Prayer (JHOP). Thank God for concerned, obedient men and women who do pray, sometimes even unceasingly.

But the question that persists is where is the travailing Church today? Oh, for pastors all across the nation to come to grips with the appalling need in our country and understand this could be turned around if they obeyed God's pleas to unite their people in prayer—and not just for an hour, but for even two or three days. This is the path that will lead to the outpourings we need so badly. Oh, that we would *grasp it*.

It is so distressing to look all around and not see pastors calling their congregations to unite in prayer and heed the pleas of God that we find in the book of Joel. Have you seen any pastors doing this? Honestly, I haven't. Have you experienced it in your church or your city? God could not be clearer in His pleading for us to do so, and it's heartbreaking that His anointed leaders are not calling their people to unite for days of prayer with fasting for our nation. How is it possible that so many don't respond to His deeply moving call to *"gird yourselves, and lament, ye priests: howl, ye ministers of the altar: come, lie all night in sackcloth, ye ministers of my God"* (Joel 1:3)?

Oh, for the day—and soon—when pastors all across the nation, together with their congregations, will fall on their knees and weep for the lost and travail for the nation. What a glorious day that will be! That will be when—and only when—the desperately needed outpouring of the Spirit will happen. Oh, for a deep, deep sense of urgency to grip our hearts and literally drive us to our knees—and then experience His promised move that we so urgently need.

Let us rejoice for those who are now standing in the gap as did Moses of old, pleading for God to forgive His people. But let us recognize it is absolutely imperative for God's people in congregations all across the nation to gather in their churches and cry out with one mighty voice, repenting for their sinfulness and pleading for another nationwide outpouring of His Spirit. Oh, intercessors, let us pray unceasingly that churches everywhere will truly grasp the absolute necessity and importance of God's people gathering in solemn assemblies to weep in repentance for their nation's evils and to cry out for that nationwide blessing. God can do it, and He will. That is His heart...but only *if and when* we meet His clearly defined conditions as spelled out in Joel. Thank God.

Chapter 3

AS IN THE DAYS OF

NOAH

IN GENESIS 6:5–7, we read these deeply disturbing words about what was occurring during Noah's day: *"God saw that the wickedness of man was great in the earth, and that every imagination of the thoughts of his heart was only evil continually. And it repented the LORD that he had made man on the earth, and it grieved him at his heart. And the LORD said, 'I will destroy man whom I have created from the face of the earth.'"* This raises a profoundly serious question: is America about to arrive at this place as well? What a terrifying thought! Oh, Lord, help us!

The Genesis passage is a tragic commentary on the corrupt state of mankind that existed in Noah's day. There was unbridled, unending wickedness and absolutely no hope of it ever changing—only getting more vile. Only Noah, his three sons, and their wives—a total of eight—knew and served the Lord. What a dark time when evil reigned unchecked on Earth, and how it grieved the Lord, the

Creator. It was then that He concluded He must *destroy them all*. Stunning, isn't it? They had become committed to evil and had crossed that line of no repentance. The Almighty knew they never would repent or turn from their wicked ways, hence His declaration.

This was further evidenced by the fact that during those 100 years while Noah and his sons were building the ark, they constantly warned the people about the coming flood that would destroy them. But all the people did was mock them, calling them fools and pipe dreamers. They certainly seemed to be so. Just think of it—building a huge ark on dry land. We also need to understand that it had never rained. So, they had never seen rain, let alone heard of rains that would cause a flood.

This is why they jeered, laughed at and mocked Noah unceasingly—for 100 long years. Without a doubt, Noah and his family were the talk of the entire known world. Daily, the people laughed them to scorn, saying, "How stupid for you to believe you heard from God and think He told you He was going to destroy everyone with a flood. Absolutely ridiculous." Nonetheless, Noah, the preacher, never stopped pleading with the people. He did so all the more when the ark was completed and standing there big and tall on dry ground. What a sight that must have been—that huge ark sitting there so far from the sea. Truthfully, to these godless men it definitely was ridiculous—no, stupid. None of us can deny that.

But the day came when what Noah had been warning about began to occur. Imagine the jeering crowds watching, totally puzzled, while animals of every strain began heading for that ark. What an incredible, unexplainable phenomenon. "What's happening?" some would have asked, beginning to feel concern. "Could Noah possibly have been right? What if he really had been instructed by God?"

Of course, many people would have begun to have such uneasy feelings, thinking, *Perhaps there was something to old man Noah's story after all!* This was all the more so as the sky grew dark with ominous black, threatening clouds, which was something they never had seen before. Then it began to rain heavily, just as Noah's family had said it would. It was all coming true. It must have been absolutely terrifying, for the rain never stopped day after day for forty long days.

Finally, the floodwaters rolled in, causing that huge ark to float. At this point, all the scoffing stopped. Now the masses trembled with terror, sensing paralyzing hopelessness and agonizing despair. Noah had been right. God had spoken. He had warned them. Oh, why, why had they not listened…not believed him?

Now all the people were overtaken with stark terror, knowing that Noah had been right. "Oh, why didn't we listen?" they would have wailed as they headed for the ark, crying out to be allowed on board. But it was too late. God Himself had shut the doors, in spite of the piercing cries and wailing of the masses doomed to die. It must have been awful. It was God's judgment, His divine wrath, always is when men don't heed His warnings through His servants to repent.

This is a terrifying, yet true story. The reason why I am sharing it is that today God has His "Noahs"—His faithful folks who are proclaiming daily about the coming divine judgment on extremely wicked and corrupt America. Sadly, as in Noah's day, their numbers are few, but their message is true. I know of some of these people. Here in California, these anointed servants of the Almighty stand in strategic places (such as crowded beaches, parks, stadiums, and farmer's markets) and, with great courage and compassion, warn people of coming divine wrath. They plead for all to repent and respond to God's plan of salvation through Christ, God's ark of safety and salvation today. Day after day, week after week, they faithfully warn the masses, pleading with them to hear and repent of their wickedness, exactly as Noah and his sons did thousands of years ago.

Almost always, when the people in America hear these warnings, they—like the people in Noah's day—jeer, mock, and rail at them. Sometimes they even threaten the street preachers. They reject the vital message from the Almighty with sneers and mocking. Sadly, none respond to accept Christ. That's right to my knowledge—not one. How shocking and sad. Day after day, week after week, these faithful heralds of truth courageously continue pleading with the masses—and, exactly as in the days of Noah, the people reject the message. *This is occurring in our society today.*

So the question persists: could it be that vast numbers of people in America are as hard and unreachable as the masses were in Noah's time? Just think of it. Today, most are so hardened spiritually that God's warnings don't even begin to move them. Rather, they mock and laugh. So it seems that *today*—here in America—there is a tragic resemblance to the corrupt state of mankind in Noah's day. How deeply concerned we, Christ's followers, should be.

What a dark, evil time it was back in Noah's day, and what a dark and evil time it is today. Just think of how this grieves the Lord, and how it should grieve us as well. It should cause us to remember our Lord's warnings of the end times, when He says, *"When the Son of man cometh, shall he find faith on the earth?"* (Luke 18:8). Are we there now? Or almost there? Hopefully not quite yet, but it does seem that we are quickly approaching that dark and corrupt state. This is profoundly serious, and it should move every true follower of Christ.

From our hearts, we should be crying, "Rather than sending Your judgment in divine, righteous wrath on us, O Lord, our hearts cry out for the glorious outpourings of Your Spirit. We cry out for Your very presence so that the masses will cry out in repentance and millions will be brought into the Kingdom—gloriously and mercifully saved! Yes, Lord, yes!"

This has happened in our history as a nation, and it was always in direct response to the heart cries of travailing men and women and powerfully anointed revivalists. Their message was heard—finally. It was awesome. Evil and wicked men, smitten by the power of God's presence, would cry out for mercy. Many would fall to the ground, later to rise as new creatures in Christ Jesus. And, gloriously, the nation was turned around. Millions repented, turned from godlessness, and came back to loving and serving the Lord. America was delivered. This has occurred not once but many times. Oh, that it may happen again…today…this year!

Chapter 4

WHAT? COULD YE NOT WATCH WITH ME ONE HOUR?

THE ETERNAL DESTINY of every human being—including you and me—was at stake. There never was nor will there ever be a fiercer battle in the heavenlies. Every demon was there in full battle array, purposing to win this epic conflict of the ages. None of us can even begin to comprehend the appalling darkness of the virtually countless vile demons that were amassed there—in Gethsemane—that crucial night as our precious Lord Jesus agonized in His body and spirit. There was war in the heavenlies, and right there in the Garden as well. Led by Lucifer himself, his vast army of followers had but one goal: to defeat the God-man, Jesus, and thereby seal the eternal doom of all mankind. They were fierce. They were relentless. They were united.

Our beloved Lord Jesus was in unimaginable agony of soul as He lay flat on His face on the ground, groaning and sweating blood. He was fighting those hordes of demons all alone, valiantly warring to not give in and avoid the terrible cross that loomed before Him. In His humanity, He was cruelly being tested to not go to the cross. His pain was so excruciating that He actually did plead momentarily, *"O my Father, if it be possible, let this cup [of unimaginable and never-before encountered travail of soul] pass from me"* (Matt. 26:39).

Just think of it: He was at the point of surrendering, it seems, to the thought of not going through with the cross. What a terrifying moment for all humanity. We know, oh so well, that if our Lord had not gone to that cross, every one of us would have been lost for eternity with absolutely no hope of forgiveness and heaven. All the demons of hell knew that as well, which is why they were so unmerciful and relentless in attacking our precious Lord Jesus. Oh, how they railed on Him, attacked Him, and undoubtedly, reminded Him constantly of all the glories of heaven that He had left.

But, thank God, Jesus overcame and defeated every vile demon. He went to that horrible cross for us and chose that path because He loved us. There are no words that could ever adequately express the gratitude we should feel.

But now we come to the convicting words that our Lord Jesus spoke to His beloved disciples that night. Why do you think our Lord took them to that garden with Him? The answer is simple: He knew full well the horrendous spiritual battle that He would face, and He longed for their prayer support. How it would have helped Him in that hour of unparalleled crisis for all humanity.

But what happened? After agonizing alone perhaps for hours, Jesus slipped back to where He had left his disciples, hoping, no doubt, they were praying. But they were fast asleep, seemingly unaware not only of the tremendous spiritual conflict that was taking place all around them but also the great importance of their prayers. Just think of the years they had heard Him ministering and had observed Him praying day after day. Remember that day they had asked Him, "Lord, teach us to pray"?

Remember, too, that after He had returned once and found them asleep, the next time He returned He found them asleep again. So it is clear they were not comprehending the colossal spiritual crisis that was happening that night. How stunning and indescribably sad, especially to Jesus whom they loved so much.

One wonders how it was possible that they could have been so oblivious to what was happening on that most eventful night. It is even more incredible when one realizes that they saw their beloved Lord sweating blood, a powerful indicator of a fierce spiritual battle. Surely they must have sensed the horrible presence of evil there in Gethsemane at least to some degree and wondered when they saw their Lord's face so contorted in indescribable anguish and pain. After all, they had been with Jesus for three years and had seen all the miracles He had performed and heard His teaching. But, it seems they did not.

It appears the vital part they could have played in uniting with Jesus against those powers of darkness never really gripped them. Is it not true, as well, that He had plainly told them over and over what was going to happen that night? Yet even in spite of that, they still didn't get it. How sad.

It was then that our Lord, looking at them with great sorrow of heart and disappointment, said those burning words: *"What? Could ye not watch with me one hour?"* (Matt. 26:40). No doubt those words burned indelibly into their hearts. How could they ever forget them? Utterly impossible. Not those three—Peter, James, and John. That's why later, after Pentecost, when great numbers came to Christ, they appointed deacons to run the business. Remembering that memorable night in Gethsemane, they declared, *"We will give ourselves continually to prayer, and to the ministry of the word"* (Acts 6:4). And they did. Prayer—constant prayer—was now a top priority in their lives and ministry. Hallelujah!

Today, in remembering Gethsemane, let us not just read this story but grasp its utmost importance. It has a powerful message for us today, and it's imperative that we think it through and understand its lesson; namely, the importance of our prayers. Could it be that today—yes, right now—our Lord is saying to us with the same disappointment and pain as He said to His disciples that night in Gethsemane, "What, can you not watch with Me one hour!?"

That night in Gethsemane was a crucial hour, but today we are also living in a critical hour in America. We see the unbelievable level of evil that is triumphing everywhere. Masses of people are totally enmeshed in the horrible grip of Lucifer and his hordes of demons. All are headed for hell and eternal damnation. The vile prince of America is utterly gleeful, together with his demonic followers, for they are winning the battle for the soul of America. A huge percentage of this nation's souls are in their grip and control. Tragically, that includes the majority of our youth, who have been swallowed into their rivers of lies and filth.

Nor does it stop there. These demonic hordes have no fear of the Church of Jesus Christ, because in most of God's houses they are preaching a watered-down gospel, and many professing Christians are believing their lies from hell. But the biggest reason for their vile glee is that on most fronts they are winning. Like the disciples of old, those in the Church do not fully understand the epic battle that is being waged or the absolute importance of their prayers. Hear it, Church. Listen, people of God.

The eternal destiny of this nation hinges on our prayers—yours, mine, and everyone's in the Church. If only we grasped this fact. Is not our Lord even now saying with a broken, bleeding heart, "Church! What? Can you not watch with Me one hour?" Sadly—no, better said, tragically—it seems that we cannot. Why? Because in most of God's houses, travailing prayer is not happening. In most of God's houses, the old-fashioned midweek prayer meetings are history. How sickening. And there are definitely no *days of prayer* taking place when God's people gather to travail for their city and the nation's lost.

Can't you hear our Lord Jesus saying, *"What, can you not watch with Me for one hour?"* Oh, Church, hear Him! Let's heed His voice!

Chapter 5

BIND THE STRONG

MAN ... NOW!

M OST OF US are aghast at the success of our wicked and guileful enemy. In fact, it's hard for us to fully comprehend the extent of the take-over that is occurring right before our eyes here in America. Unabashedly, too. It's mindboggling and even terrifying.

It's essential that we grasp what has happened in our beloved Christian America! Of course, maybe we should say what is happening in what *was* Christian America. Let me explain. It usually is estimated that today there are approximately 60,000,000 Christians now in America. That sounds great, yes, but if that is so, it means 80% of our population doesn't know the Lord! That's 240,000,000 who don't know the Lord! How appalling! That's the reason why I say, "what was Christian America.

Is this not made apparent by the fact that the percentage of divorces among Christians is higher than among non-Christians? Now that is really sad. Or the absolutely distressing report that we referred to earlier about how a high percentage of our pastors—thirty percent or more—are hooked on pornography? With this being the case, what percentage of Christians and our young people would also not fall into this category? We could go on and on. What is occurring is tragic beyond words.

Another extremely sickening fact is that a majority of America's youth have swallowed hook, line, and sinker the evil lies of evolution that have been propagated through "evangelists of hell" such as Karl Marx, Sigmund Freud, Friedrich Nietzsche, Richard Dawkins, and Christopher Hitchens, to mention just a few. Believe it or not, for the last three generations and more, these lies have been sweeping into our schools and into the media. If we but realized the current state of America, we would comprehend we are now primarily a non-Bible believing nation—which is a far, far cry from that of our godly founding fathers.

Some may challenge this statement, but current estimates reveal that there are approximately sixty million Christians in our nation today. That sounds like a large number at first, but our population is more than 300 million. That means that only twenty percent of Americans are Christians. That's one in five, a small minority. Is that not profoundly disturbing and, hopefully, something that will drive us to our knees in prayer? In the early days of our history, the Bible was used as a textbook, but today it is called the "hate book" and is considered something to be feared and not believed.

Our enemy has another army of "evangelists" who are also deceiving many across the nation. These are propaga- tors of the many cults that have succeeded in ensnaring millions. Oh, how tragic. The enemy is triumphing on so many fronts today. Oh, that we may pray for the lost souls in our land and seek to win them to true faith in our precious Lord Jesus. That is our calling as the followers of Christ, who alone is the truth, the way, and the life.

My heart bleeds with grief and pain as I see the children of even strong church members—including elders' and pastors' children—falling from the faith and believing the lies of Satan. Truthfully, this hits home for many of us, doesn't it? Many of these children not only argue for their beliefs in evolution—and their disbelief in God's Word—but some even scornfully laugh at their godly parents or grandparents. While they may respect their parents, who they know are genuine in their faith, it stops there. Believe in the Bible or Jesus Christ? They want none of it. They've been told the Bible is "mere myth and untrue" countless times throughout their school years.

Beloved, if we but comprehended the percentage of America's people today who have swallowed these deceptions of the enemy, we would be aghast. These are the ones who have been elected and are leading our nation down a path that is fundamentally different from what it once was. We should be concerned about this—to the point of taking action. Truly, we are in a war with the powers of darkness for America's soul. Tragically, we are losing big time, almost by default.

What should our response be? Throw up our hands in despair and lay down our weapons of warfare? Certainly not! Never! Instead, we need to take up our weapons and use them to win back America and defeat our vile enemy and his army of demons. We can bind the strong man and cast out the enemy in Jesus' almighty name. We will win, for we are *"more than conquerors through [Christ] that loved us"* (Rom. 8:37). However, we must understand that this will be a fierce fight and no easy win.

As Paul stated in 2 Corinthians 10:4-6, *"The weapons of our warfare are not carnal, but mighty through God to the pulling down of strong holds [Satan's]; casting down imaginations, and every high thing that exalteth itself against the knowledge of God, and bringing into captivity every thought to the obedience of Christ; and having in a readiness to revenged all disobedience."* This is war. We are deeply enmeshed in the battle of the ages for America's very future: our youth and our children. That is a solemn fact. Wake up, Christians in America. We have to totally rout the enemy. If we don't, we will be destroyed.

So let's heed our Lord's clear-cut orders in Ephesians 6, for there is no way we can misunderstand them: *"Put on the whole armour of God...for we wrestle not against flesh and blood, but against principalities, against powers, against the rulers of the darkness of this world, against spiritual wickedness in high places. Wherefore take unto you the whole armour of God, that ye may be able to withstand in the evil day [that day exists now, here in America]....Above all, taking the shield of faith, wherewith ye shall be able to quench all the fiery darts of the wicked [all Satan's lies].... And take the helmet of salvation, and the sword of the Spirit, which is the word of God: praying always and with all prayer and supplication in the Spirit, and watching thereto with all perseverance"* (vv. 11-13,16-18).

We should expect to win—in Jesus' name. For we are more than conquerors through Him who loves us. *"Now thanks be unto God, which always causeth us to triumph in Christ, and maketh manifest the savour of his knowledge by us in every place"* (2 Cor. 2:14). That spells certain victory. We can win, and we must win. And together, with all of us uniting—and with our victorious almighty Lord Jesus—we *will* win.

This battle has reached epic proportions in America today, and we must do our warfare on our knees, standing on Christ's promises. Tragically, thus far, the Church has failed in this regard, for there has been a terrible dearth of prayer throughout most churches in Christian America. Prayer is our mightiest and most effective weapon in this war against the powers of darkness, and by using it along with God's Word—our sword—we can conquer our demonic foes. Hallelujah! That's a fact. This battle will be won on our knees.

It is imperative we have clear expectation of what we need to do: take back every bit of territory that we have lost. Nothing less is acceptable. This means Christians nationwide need to get back on the school boards, be directly involved in our school system, and root out the erroneous teachings of evolution. "Can't" is not in our vocabulary. Above all, we must remember that our victory is certain because our leader is none other than Jesus Christ, Lord of the universe. Since He is leading us, victory is certain. Yes, it will be a hard battle, and it will take time, but we must never lose our focus or give up. Glory to God!

Chapter 6

WHY?

G IVEN THIS ESCALATING evil and appalling
spiritual decadence in our nation, why do we see
such astounding lukewarmness in the Church?
Why are there no alarms being set off or passionate calls to
prayer and repentance by churches everywhere? This burning question cries for an answer. Why aren't there at least
some—if even only a few—who are lifting up their voices
and calling the nation's lost to repent? Why? I'm perplexed
and puzzled. My very being searches for the answer.

Brothers and sisters, prayerfully think with me about
this. How many pastors do you know who, like Nehemiah of
old when he heard about the terrible situation in Jerusalem,
simply could not eat and spent hours—no, days—crying
out to God in agony of soul for his people? With tears he
pled for the Lord to deliver his people! What about Daniel,
a captive in Babylon far from home? You can just picture
him on his knees fasting for days because his burden is so

great. Oh, how these men brokenheartedly repented for the terrible wickedness of their people, pleading for their forgiveness and restoration.

These men's burden for their people was so consuming they couldn't even eat. Daniel was prime minister of that vast empire with unimaginable demands on his time, yet that did not stop him from making time to travail for his people. What examples they are to us. Oh, for some Nehemiahs and Daniels in America today—men so spiritually keen and sensitive to the tugs of the Spirit and the needs of their people that they respond in prayer not just for an hour but also for days and even weeks.

Wouldn't it be incredible if we found among us here in sin-sick America those who were so burdened that they, too, could not eat but simply made time to repent and cry out to the Lord for days on end? Why aren't we seeing congregations of God's people setting aside days for fasting and praying passionately for the countless millions of precious Americans who are living in flagrant sin? Don't we see where America is headed and the dark clouds of divine wrath that are looming on the horizon? We must weep with broken hearts, pleading for our God to forgive our people and restore them to spiritual wholeness.

Hear Jeremiah as he weeps for Israel, crying, "*My bowels, my bowels! I am pained at my very heart; my heart maketh a noise in me; I cannot hold my peace, because thou hast heard, O my soul, the sound of the trumpet, the alarm of war....Oh that my head were waters, and mine eyes a fountain of tears, that I might weep day and night for the slain of the daughter of my people*" (Jer. 4:19; 9:1). Now that is carrying a burden.

How that man agonized for his people and travailed in unceasing prayer!

If we love our homeland with the love of Christ, shouldn't there be at least some among us who, like Jeremiah, are being moved with that same divinely imparted compassion for the millions of people in our nation who are entrapped in unending evils? We are concerned, maybe, but not heartbroken or weeping before the Lord to rescue us from the evils and the direction we're headed. Oh, that many will travail with tears, repent for America and plead for the desperately needed visitation of the Almighty.

Perhaps you have read about David Brainerd, who was often so moved of the Spirit in his burden for America's Indians that he would slip off his horse and travail for such long hours during the winter months that the snow around him would melt. Now that is intercession. That is being burdened for the lost. His prayer burden was so heavy that he was oblivious to the wet or the bitter cold—nothing else seemed to matter. No wonder the Spirit of God moved mightily, sweeping many native Americans into the kingdom of God.

STIR ME, LORD
Stir me, oh, stir me, Lord, till all my heart
Is filled with strong compassion
For these souls!
Till Thy constraining love reach
To the poles...
Far north and south in burning deep desire,
Till east and west are caught in love's
Great fire!

Stir me, oh, stir me, Lord, till prayer is pain,
Till prayer is joy, till prayer
Turn to praise!
Stir me till heart and will and mind, yes, all
Is wholly Thine to use through
All my days!
Stir till I learn to pray "exceedingly,"
Stir till I learn to wait "expectantly."

Stir me, oh, stir me, Lord! Thy heart was stirred
By love's intensest fire, till Thou didst give
Thy only Son, Thy best beloved One
E'en to the dreadful cross
That I might live!
Stir me to give myself so back to thee
That Thou canst give thyself
Again through me!

Stir me, oh, stir me, Lord, for I can see
Thy glorious triumph day begin to break
The dawn already guilds the eastern sky!
Oh, Church of Christ, arise, awake! Awake!
Oh, stir us, Lord as heralds of that day,
For the night is past!
The king is on His way!

Chapter 7

POLITICAL?

NOT REALLY!

PASTORS HAVE BEEN hoodwinked into believing that by getting involved in the issues happening all across our nation, they are engaging in politics. So they refuse to speak up or get involved. Is this not serious? Is it not a fact that if we say or do nothing, before long our Christian nation will become a socialist, non-Christian state? Shouldn't that move us to action so we can remain a Bible-believing and worldwide-gospel-propagating people?

This may shock and offend some people—especially pastors. But the truth is that many of the issues we face today are truly spiritual issues. When evil triumphs, as Christ's followers, we have to speak up and fight for what is right. We cannot allow evil and corruption to win. Never! Nor can we stay silent or uninvolved. Keeping quiet and taking no action is wrong—we could even say sinful—and those who choose to say nothing or allow evil to win are guilty. We don't want to get to that place, but we have done nothing to prevent it thus far. Silence has been the accepted response in recent days in the face of relentless attacks on the teachings of God's Word, our standard of truth and living.

Why has the Church been virtually silent and inactive regarding the takeover of our schools? Why have we allowed wicked people whose goal is to wipe out Christianity and make America a godless nation of evolutionists and atheists infiltrate our institutions? It's appalling and wrong. What's the real explanation? Fear. We have been afraid to speak up and stand up for what we believe is right. We have been afraid to fight in defense of our nation's children. Now we are reaping what we have sown through our fear and compromise. Who today is leading our nation to hell, socialism and maybe even Nazism? The graduates of our schools! We have not united, O Church of Jesus Christ, to fight and win these unending inroads of evil.

Is it not a fact that our silence—our lack of taking courageous, persistent action to fight these advances—has allowed them to win? We could have won, and we should have on every front. We still can, for the Almighty is on our side, but it will be a fierce battle. As Christ's followers, we never have to lose in these skirmishes. Oh, for the Church of Jesus Christ to take back the territory it has lost. Oh, for someone to lead us back to the biblical roots that our godly, Jesus-fearing founders established.

There will be a price to pay for our apathy—that is a given. It is imperative that we never forget the tremendous price our founding fathers paid to win our freedom so we could follow the teachings of God's Word and establish a Christian republic. Sadly, most of us have taken these precious freedoms for granted. Is it not a fact that the majority of our founding fathers lost virtually everything in their struggle? Many even lost their lives. We've reaped countless benefits because they decided to take action and stand for their beliefs.

Today it is our turn, pastors and fellow Christians. While it is true we can expect to suffer in varying degrees, that is never a reason for backing out or doing and saying nothing. It's absolutely essential we do something to win back our religious freedoms not only for our own blessing but also for our posterity as well as our continued witness to proclaim Christ to the world's perishing millions. Rejoice, but understand this: our enemy is desperate to stop our witness.

Most of us are aware of the almost total capitulation of the Church in Germany during the Nazi regime due to fear and a misinterpretation of Romans 13. They went silent and didn't take a stand for the truth, and indescribable evil won in that nation. Not only were six and a half million Jews murdered, but millions of the elderly, the ill, and the homeless also vanished. This is a powerful illustration that still exists in the living memory of many people today. The lesson? When the Church is silent—when it doesn't take a unified, courageous stand for the truth and for God's Word—it and many others will suffer for it.

We don't want anything even close to that to happen here in America. However, it seems we are starting down that path and similar things could happen here in the not too distant future if we continue to compromise—say nothing—and not take a clear, courageous stand with no intention of giving in or losing. We can be sure the Church in Germany under Hitler never dreamed what ultimately occurred would happen in their nation. Remember Hitler was immensely popular and that he deceived millions. Church in America, it is vital we learn from their silence.

I do not enjoy being the whistleblower, but when I see what is looming on the horizon in my beloved America, I know it is wrong to stay silent. Today, a number of people in our country are also seeing the direction we are being led—or, we should say, being forced to go. Fear has gripped the hearts of millions. However, others are so lost in just living that they are oblivious to the perils that are coming our way. We must understand that saying nothing or doing nothing—especially for Christian leaders and pastors—is *not* an option. Our calling is to be the salt that prevents decay and corruption.

Pastors, please pray this through. Let's seriously ask the Lord to lead us in how we can take action and be vital players in this drama for the souls and future of Christian America, as well as the eternal destiny of millions around the world. Let's be courageous and urge our congregations to cry out against these inroads of corruption with one mighty voice. Oh, for the godly courage to proclaim the standards of God's Word at any cost. Yes, there will be a price to pay. Some will be arrested, and the day is coming when some will be killed for standing strong and tall. Our Lord has said so in His final discourse of the end times with His disciples (see Mark 13).

Thank God for the Tea Parties. Many among us are now speaking up boldly to expose the ways in which our current administration has been misleading us. Many of these individuals, without a doubt, are followers of Christ. They are mobilizing, speaking up and taking a stand. They are letting their light shine.

Understand that as God's people, we must boldly communicate with our nation's leaders and call them to stop this march toward socialism and atheism. So bombard Congress with letters and phone calls. Join the rallies. Speak up! Stand up tall! Become an active member of God's army today with the singular goal of winning America back to its godly, Bible-believing roots, and pray unceasingly for all of our Christian leaders who are leading this fight. Begin today, and never give up or doubt that we will win. *"Fight the good fight of faith"* (1 Tim. 6:12)! This is war—real war.

Thanks be unto God, which always causeth us to triumph in Christ, and maketh manifest the savour of his knowledge by us in every place. For we are unto God a sweet savour of Christ, in them that are saved, and in them that perish: To the one we are the savour of death unto death; and to the other savour of life unto life" (2 Cor. 2:14-16).

Chapter 8

THEY ARE WINNING!

GET READY FOR a real shock: the followers of Islam are definitely planning to take over our beloved homeland, America, and ultimately force us to bow the knee to their faith—their god, Allah! Is this not an ominous sign? None of us want this to happen, yet most Americans—Christians included—are seemingly oblivious to the fact this is occurring. It is also happening in Europe and in Canada as well. This is why it is imperative that we, the followers of Christ, wake up and see what is taking place before our very eyes and take action to stop the spread of Islam in our country.

Don't be like most Americans who think: *Impossible! This could never happen here in Christian America!* If you feel this way, I am sorry to have to say that you are mistaken in your thinking—it breaks my heart to have to say it. It is happening right now...today...every day. The followers of Islam have no doubts about winning our nation to their faith. What is even more shocking is their unabashed boldness. So far, they have been winning each phase of the conquest exactly as they have planned. They are right on target. At the very latest, by 2020—less than ten years away—they fully expect to accomplish that goal and make America an Islamic nation.

How is it Muslims are so assured of success? Perhaps the question we should ask is why they *shouldn't* feel so assured, as they have succeeded every step of the way so far. Their plans have gone off without a hitch. And hear this, O Church of Jesus Christ: by turning a blind eye to the situation, we have allowed them to succeed. Even more serious, we in the Church have showed no concern about their multiple inroads into America. They have more than 100 mosques in New York alone. We have all seen pictures on the Internet of great numbers of Muslims kneeling on the streets, stopping all traffic—and getting away with it. And we hear not a peep from the Christian community.

What about Muslim groups unashamedly seeking to buy property *right next to Ground Zero* in New York? They want to build a huge mosque there that, without a doubt, would symbolize their victory in the United States. That's stunning! Let's not forget they murdered 3,000 Americans on that spot. They fully expect to build the mosque there, and why shouldn't they believe they will succeed? We in the Church, essentially, have been unconcerned. But we should be, and passionately so. Every follower of Jesus Christ should lift his or her voice in insistent protest. Have you? I have. Thank God a few others have, but this still only represents a mere handful of faithful, valiant soldiers of Jesus Christ.

If the Muslims had tried to infiltrate our nation a century ago, there would have been a nationwide uproar stopping it. But not today. Most Christians in America are preoccupied with just living instead of being true soldiers of the cross who mobilize to stop such takeovers—at any cost. Beloved, understand this: our country is the special target of the enemy because it is from our shores that countless followers of Jesus Christ have covered the globe, taking the good news of salvation to every nation and people. Satan, our real enemy, is filled with indescribable rage at us, and he has one intent: to take Christian America down.

He is using the followers of Islam—who, sadly, unknowingly serve him—to accomplish this feat. Please, come to grips with the reality that it is actually happening right now. *Now* is the time to take action, Church. Now is the time to mobilize. Now is the time to love them into the kingdom of God. Travail in prayer for our Almighty God to send the desperately needed—and promised—fourth awakening that will restore America to its Christian roots and convert millions of precious Muslims in our nation to Christ. Wouldn't that be an awesome turnaround? Think big. Think God.

In Isaiah 55:9, God Himself proclaims, *"For as the heavens are higher than the earth, so are my ways higher than your ways, and my thoughts than your thoughts."* Glory. Rejoice. God can pour out His Spirit on Muslims as well, sweeping countless of their numbers into the Kingdom. It can happen, and it must happen. Remember God is on our side, and we can be absolutely sure that He longs to earnestly come down in such glory and power that even many in the Islamic faith in the United States will be won to Christ. This thought gives one goose bumps! *"With men this is impossible; but with God all things are possible"* (Matt. 19:26). Shout it from the rooftops.

Beloved, our hearts must cry, "God, awaken us to action—to passionate praying and mobilizing so we can turn this onslaught around and win millions of these precious, Satan-deceived people to Christ." Now, that's what our Lord wants. Our Lord Jesus is the Lord of the universe, and every demon trembles at the mention of His name. Even Lucifer himself trembles. Fellow Christians, understand God has brought the threat of Islam to our nation not for it to overcome us, but for us to win those who practice Islam to Christ. He alone is the Savior of mankind, and this includes all the Muslims about us in our nation. Hallelujah!

Chapter 9

WHAT ARE WE DOING
TO WIN THE LOST?

OUR LORD JESUS says, *"Ye have not chosen me, but I have chosen you, and ordained you, that ye should go and bring forth fruit"* (John 15:16). In the very same discourse, He warns, *"Every branch in me that beareth not fruit he taketh away"* (John 15:1). Frankly, this verse should challenge us, for it is a serious warning. Most assuredly, Christ expects us to win souls. The burning question is whether we are winning these souls for Christ today.

How many souls have you or your church led to the Lord recently? That is our purpose for being here. It is why the Lord led you to where you live—to pray for every precious, perishing neighbor and to seek to point him or her to the Savior. Fellow Christian, do you prayer walk your neighborhood or other needy areas of your town or city? Have you ever considered having Bible studies in your home to share the Lord Jesus? Each of us needs to grasp this: we are not living where we are by mere chance—God put us there to be a witness for Christ and point every neighbor to Him. Here's something for us to seriously think about: on Judgment Day, we don't want our unsaved neighbors asking, "Why didn't you tell us about Christ?"

I recall an amazing testimony of a vibrant Christian lady in Yamagata City, Japan, who was a saleswoman for Shiseido cosmetic products. She said, "I've discovered that every woman is hurting with family problems and deep hurts, but most have no one whom they can really confide in. I have products on my shelves, but I never have to do a sales talk. Each woman, upon discovering that I am someone they can confide in, opens up and shares her heartaches. It's then that I can show love and the blessedness of knowing Jesus, and they always listen! Invariably, they buy my products." Truly, that home is an evangelism center. Hallelujah!

What about you, fellow Christian? Do you have a burden for your neighbors...for your town and city? I suggest you make a list of your neighbors and others to whom you've witnessed and faithfully pray for them *by name*. Again, my mind goes back to Japan. When we were pioneering our first new church, a young Bible School student came for a summer to work with us. One day after she had been there for only a short time, I dropped by on business and discovered she already had the names of every person in our church and her unsaved neighbors posted on her walls. Why? So she could pray over each one by name—each day. That's a soul winner. That girl taught me a lifelong lesson.

Now consider this testimony of a true soul-winner here in America. One Sunday, a pastor kindly invited me to his home for lunch after I had shared the message that morning in his church. I sauntered over to the house ahead of him, but on entering I was stunned to see an unusually large dining room table and large-sized serving bowls. Fascinated, I asked, "Brother, why is everything here on the table so big?" I will never forget his beaming reply. With joy he responded, "My brother, I have led more people to Christ around this table than I have at the church altar!" I assure you, the impact of that powerful testimony still reverberates in my heart. The lesson? Every Christian's home should be a soul-winning center. How convicting and inspiring.

In Romans 12 we read, *"He that giveth, let him do it with simplicity…distributing to the necessity of saints; given to hospitality"* (vv. 8,13). Truly, if the Lord had His way in our lives, our homes would be centers of unceasing ministries. They would be centers of multiple ministries such as prayer meetings, Bible studies, sharing Jesus with neighbors and friends, and entertaining evangelists, missionaries, and even homeless people. In Isaiah 58:6-7, the prophet wrote, *"Is not this the fast that I have chosen…to deal thy bread to the hungry, and that thou bring the poor that are cast out to thy house? When thou seest the naked, that thou cover him; and that thou hide not thyself from thine own flesh"?* Our Lord Himself said, *"For I was an hungered, and ye gave me meat: I was thirsty, and ye gave me drink: I was a stranger, and ye took me in: naked, and ye clothed me.…Verily I say unto you, Inasmuch as ye have done it unto one of the least of these my brethren, ye have done it unto me"*(Matt. 25:35-36,45). Is it not a fact that if we, the Lord's children, lived up to the expectations of our Lord, we would be doing a lot more to impact more people for Christ in our homes?

Sadly, such is not the norm these days. Most of us hurry home and shut the door on opportunities to bless others—and this in spite of the fact that most of us today have larger and better facilities than they did in the past. Shame on us! Oh, that our homes might be centers of ministry—our very own ministry with God using us to bless others and win lost souls. Oh, that we would take the time to invite our neighbors—one at a time—for a cup of coffee or a meal and develop deeper friendships with them, and this would ultimately lead us to sharing the joy of our Lord Jesus with them. *God has put each of us where we are to be His witnesses.* Wouldn't it be incredible if the day came when we were having Bible studies regularly in our homes and our precious neighbors were coming to Christ? Glory!

There is something else that distresses me greatly: why is it that we always see the propagators of false cults zealously going door to door and winning many people to their faith, but we seldom, if ever, see Christians out there witnessing? What's the real reason? Is it that Christians are afraid to go out and share their faith, or is it simply they aren't that concerned? Shouldn't members of every evangelical church be making the time to share the good news with every person in their city? Sadly, this is not happening. I heard one pastor once say that whenever he got out into the community, they always had new people coming into his church, but when he stopped no new people would come. That says something, doesn't it?

Frankly, I often think of Judgment Day, when we will all stand before the Almighty and countless precious souls—some of whom were our neighbors and unsaved friends—will all be headed for a lost eternity. They will point their fingers at us and wail, "Oh, why, why didn't you tell us?" Their cry, as Psalm 142:4 states, is so impacting: *"I looked on my right hand, and beheld, but there was no man that would know me...no man cared for my soul."* How important that we heed our Lord's poignant warning in Ezekiel 33:7-9: *"Son of man, I have made you a watchman for the house of Israel; so hear the word I speak and give them warning from me. When I say to the wicked, 'O wicked man, you will surely die,' and you do not speak out to dissuade him from his ways, that wicked man will die for his sin, and I will hold you accountable for his blood. But if you do warn the wicked man to turn from his ways and he does not do so, he will die for his sin, but you will have delivered yourself"* (NIV).

Truthfully, I shudder whenever I read these passages, for I don't want anyone pointing his or her finger at me on Judgment Day. What about you, fellow Christian? Just think about the shame and indescribable anguish of heart you will feel when you see those whom you've known falling into hell. But that's precisely what will happen if you fail to point these individuals to the Savior while you can. Hear it, think it through and never forget it.

We know full well our primary calling as Christ's followers is to win souls—to proclaim to every man, woman and child that Jesus is the Savior of mankind. There is no other name under heaven whereby we can be saved. It is tragic for us to be so wrapped up in just living and having a good time that we do nothing to point others—neighbors, friends, relatives—to Jesus. How important it is that we live each day, each moment, with eternity's values in view. It is so easy to get so wrapped up in the cares of this life that we forget about Judgment Day.

We can't allow this truth to escape us. Even if it means ridicule or rejection by many—or worse—still, we are to preach Jesus. The Early Church certainly did, even though they suffered for it. Each one of Jesus' disciples was martyred for his witness, except Judas of course, and John, who miraculously escaped death and was exiled to Patmos. What does this tell us? Simply this: we may be ridiculed and even persecuted for our witness, but this is never a reason for us to avoid lifting up the name of Christ. And if we do suffer, we're in good company. Jesus plainly tells us we will be hated—and, truthfully, we are today. Some will even be killed. But that should not deter us from proclaiming Jesus to the unsaved. Doesn't our Lord plainly say, *"Blessed are they which are persecuted for righteousness' sake…blessed are ye, when men shall revile you, and persecute you, and shall say all manner of evil against you falsely, for my sake. Rejoice, and be exceeding glad: for great is your reward in heaven: for so persecuted they the prophets which were before you"* (Matt. 5:10-12).

I pray the Lord would move and so empower us, His followers, that beginning today all across America, countless men and women who know and love Christ would be so set on fire with a burning passion for lost souls that they would become mighty soul winners for God's glory.

I feel the following poem is very significant, as it brings into vivid focus the cry of the lost…all those perishing millions.

A hundred thousand souls a day
Are passing one by one away
In Christless guilt and gloom.
Without one ray of hope or light
With future dark as endless night—
They're passing to their doom!

O, Holy Ghost, Thy people move,
Baptize their hearts with faith and love,
And consecrate their gold
At Jesus' feet their millions pour
And all their ranks unite once more
As in the days of old!

Armies of pray'r your promise claim
Prove the full pow'r of Jesus' Name
And take the victory.
Your conq'ring Captain leads you on,
The glorious fight may still be won
This very century, this very century!

O, let us then his coming haste,
O, let us end this awful waste
Of souls that never die!
A thousand million still are lost,
A Savior's blood has paid the cost—
Oh, hear their dying cry! O hear their dying cry!

Chapter 10

IS IT RIGHT?

I N BYGONE DAYS, many of God's servants had a great burden for the lost and for their country as well. Many of them had so great a burden that it literally compelled them to go to their knees in unceasing travail of soul for those around them.

I am reminded of John Knox of Scotland, who spent countless hours on his knees crying, "Oh, God! Give me Scotland or I die!" Night after night, he was there on his knees, wrapped in a blanket, weeping for the lost of his homeland. We know the end of that story—a nationwide awakening occurred that swept multitudes into the kingdom of God and birthed the Presbyterian Church. From little Scotland, the Lord sent numerous servants to proclaim the good news around the world.

I am also reminded of my last visit to Korea. It was our final night, and our missionary guide took us to the site of an evangelistic tent campaign. The service had just finished, but there were thirty to forty believers still earnestly praying. I will never forget what our guide said: "They will continue praying all night long." What zeal for the lost. It is little wonder there are so many followers of Christ in that land. Oh, that we here in America had that kind of burden and commitment!

The story in Acts 2 should inspire and challenge us. Countless thousands of people were in Jerusalem celebrating the Passover when suddenly, emerging from an upper room, came 120 Spirit-filled followers of Christ, all mightily lifting up His glorious name. God's glory, His very presence, filled the place. There were people from every surrounding nation, and to their amazement, all of them were hearing the message in their own tongue. Then Peter stood and preached Jesus Christ and Him crucified, and 3,000 deeply convicted people were gloriously saved. That was only the beginning. From then on, countless thousands of people were swept into the Kingdom.

Was that to be the exception? Not if God has His way in our lives. It's imperative that we learn from the example of the 120 believers; namely, that this outpouring of the Spirit was preceded with their waiting on God for ten long days. We must not forget that important point. The challenge for us is to follow their example. While we may not need to pray for ten days straight as they did, we should be asking ourselves what would happen today if we fully followed their example. Don't you think there would be another mighty move of God? There is not a shadow of doubt that our God still yearns unceasingly to manifest His glory and sweep countless souls into His kingdom here in the United States.

That's a given. That's our God's heart. He is *"not willing that any should perish, but that all come to repentance"* (2 Pet. 3:9). A thousand times yes!

Almost always, I find that when Christians are attending prayer meetings, the focus of their prayers are for themselves and for the Lord to bless them more. I fully agree this is perfectly all right at times, but what presses home so heavily on my heart is this: why aren't we praying more for the lost all around us? I don't mean to be critical or judgmental, I just want to earnestly search for answers. This is a burning issue that cries out for a solution. Should we not be weeping for the perishing people "out there"? They are a majority, and virtually all of them never darken a church door because they are so enmeshed in the enemy's clutches.

Beloved fellow Christians, I am pressed in my heart to ask, *Where is our passion for the lost, all those hell-bound souls in our schools, our cities and our neighborhoods that are headed for a Christless eternity?* Oh, that we may be so burdened that we find ourselves weeping for their salvation as did John Knox and David Brainerd. Again I ask how it is possible that we seldom hear such cries for the lost? Are you with me, fellow Christian? Are you also troubled with such concerns? I trust so. Winning the lost for Christ is our responsibility as long as we are in this earth. In Proverbs 29:18 we read, *"Where there is no vision [for the lost], the people perish."* Sadly, that is all too true in America today.

There is another closely related question that also cries out for an answer. It has to do with the many Christian conferences that I see happening in major cities and on gorgeous cruise ships in the Caribbean, the Hawaiian Islands and Alaska. These are truly exotic and exciting conferences, and they always feature an array of powerful Bible teachers. Praise God! It is wonderful that so many of our fellow Christians are being blessed. But the question that keeps rising within my heart is whether the Lord would be much more pleased if those energies (and vast sums of money) were invested in gospel crusades devoted to winning the lost. Honestly, I believe He would be. Is it possible the majority of Christians today have never given this a thought? This seems to be the case, but we need to do so.

Many of us remember with great joy the good old days, when all across the nation evangelistic outreaches were the norm—in tents, in churches and often in stadiums. We recall the old sawdust trails and seeing folk flocking to the front to receive Christ. We remember those happy days when Billy Graham lifted up the name of Jesus in stadium after stadium, all filled to capacity. Oh, the thrill of seeing thousands of people stream toward the altar to receive the Lord Jesus. It was joy unspeakable.

So, why are we not seeing such crusades in our cities and in our churches today? Why do we not have the same zeal to win the lost? Have you recently seen a citywide outreach to win precious souls to Christ in your city or even in your church on a local level? Sadly, in most cases, we have to admit these are not happening. It is little wonder the numbers of the unsaved today are skyrocketing.

Church, we need to wake up and speak up. Let's get back to fulfilling our calling—to having crusades nationwide and in our churches to win the lost to Christ. Oh, that every church would become an evangelism center and every follower of Jesus Christ a soul winner. Oh, that churches all across the nation would become houses of prayer where unceasing intercession for the lost is occurring. Oh, that churches in city after city would unite in genuine unity to become one mighty voice to transform our cities into Jesus-following people. Think big. After all, with God all things are possible!

Chapter 11

WOE TO A PEOPLE
WHO OFFEND THEIR
LITTLE ONES

IT'S PROFOUNDLY IMPORTANT that we all heed our Lord's very strong warning when He says, *"Whoso shall offend one of these little ones which believe in Me! It is better for him that a millstone were hanged about his neck, and that he were drowned in the depth of the sea"* (Matt. 18:6). Does this not mean that before the Almighty, our solemn obligation is to teach children to love and serve the Lord God? Definitely so!

This also means we are to protect our children from any and all teachings contrary to God's Word. In Deuteronomy 6:7, God commands, *"Thou shalt teach them diligently unto thy children, and shall talk of them when thou sittest in thine house."* The question is whether we are doing this. Haven't we all been in great error by sending our children off to school when we know—or should know, if we're truly responsible parents—that they are being taught anti-Christian lies? That is precisely what has been happening.

How is it possible, if we are truly born-again Christians who are concerned about our children, that this has happened all across America and we have not stopped it? We could have—or, better said, we should have.

So, today, in our very own once-Christian America, our children and youth are being taught in school *not* to believe in God and instead to believe in evolution, the devil's counterfeit for the truth—a teaching that leads them not to heaven but to hell. On our college campuses, Jesus and the Bible are out. Christianity is scoffed at, and only the propagating of anti-Christian views are taught as fact. Given this, it is only logical that kids from Christian homes ultimately doubt God's Word and question whether Jesus is the Savior of the world—*"the way, the truth and the life"* (John 14:6). It is commonly estimated that approximately two-thirds of Christian young people who attend secular colleges lose their biblical faith. What a dark picture of America's youth today. We should be profoundly concerned, but are we? Seeing so little action to reverse this evil makes one wonder if today's Christians are brokenhearted over this.

We should praise God for the excellent Christian colleges and universities throughout the land. In addition, a few churches with fine Christian curriculums from pre-school through high school are training students in God's Word. But the vast majority of our public schools are bastions of atheism.

Our founding fathers were godly men who said we could never stand as a true republic apart from the Bible. In those days, the Bible was used as a textbook in our schools. It is amazing how far we have fallen, and we are really paying for it. On practically every campus, prayer and any mention of the name of Jesus is out. Nor is any display or reference to the Ten Commandments permitted, "lest they influence young people to obey them," as one of our Supreme Court justices once said. So, instead of any teaching from God's Word, our youth are taught that there is no God and that we are all here by pure chance. No design. No purpose. All this is rammed down the throats of our nation's precious kids for twelve years (sixteen if they go on to a college). No wonder our nation is filled with evolutionists and liberals. We are truly reaping what we have sown. This is also why the majority of our nation's leaders are way out in left field, far removed from any of our Christian roots, and are leading us toward socialism and worse. Now *that's* a terrifying fact.

How is it possible that Christian parents and evangelical, Bible-believing churches have allowed all this to happen? For we have—by not speaking up and stopping the enemy from taking over. Truthfully, the enemy has won by default. This is absolutely tragic and something for which we will have to answer on Judgment Day. Let's not forget that.

Why hasn't there been a nationwide outcry by God's people to prevent these inroads of corruption? The answer is because most Christians are either too fearful to do anything about it or are too busy and too uninvolved with what our children are being taught. God help us. We need to awaken to action, beginning right now. It is imperative that we do something, for the eternal welfare of millions of our children hinges on it. Doing nothing and saying nothing is *not* an option. The Bible exhorts us to *"fight the good fight of faith"* (1 Tim. 6:12). Well, that's exactly what's coming down the pike.

Allow me to add another issue that is an important piece of this scenario. In doing so, I am painfully aware this may offend some people, and if this is the case, please forgive me. Again, I do not want to be critical, I am just deeply concerned for the millions of America's children who have been left to the wolves of hell in our regular school system. Here is my issue: when we pull children from Christian homes out of the regular school system, we surrender the rest of the nation's children—which are the majority of children—to the enemy's control.

I understand why parents place their children in Christian schools, but it's imperative that we all realize what the effects are of that decision. This concern is so heavy on my heart, and I believe it is on the Lord's heart as well. When we pull our kids out of public school, we are not allowing them to be the salt and light that our Lord has called them to be. Does this not explain why most Americans today are unbelievers? Of course, there have been other powerful influences, such as TV, Internet, and movies, but none have had more influence than our school system. There really is no way to get around this disconcerting fact. It is profoundly important that we clearly see what has happened and be careful not to forget our young people in our secular schools. We must pray and take action as well.

Keep in mind there are many children from Christian families in our godless, Jesus-hating schools, and these kids are now in the minority. How they desperately need our prayers, for tragically, most of them are succumbing to the evil influences in which they are daily enmeshed. *We must not forget them.* We must pray for Christian clubs and every campus ministry that is lifting up the awesome name of our Lord Jesus on all those campuses. Likewise, it is imperative we lift up Christian teachers in the secular school system, praying that they will have the courage and wisdom to let their light shine, and even have the joy of leading young people to Christ. Let's pray that they will not, through fear, hide their witness but be led of the Spirit to shine gloriously for the Savior.

Oh, that every Christian parent—beginning with you and me—will take action and become an active member of God's army to fight the corruption and change the evil curriculum in our schools. Change is possible, but only if we unite and take action. As Paul says in Ephesians 3:20, *"Now unto him that is able to do exceeding abundantly above all that we ask or think, according to the power that worketh in us."* Again, saying nothing and doing nothing is not an option, because the eternal destiny of our children and our school systems are at stake. Furthermore, the future of our Christian nation is also at stake, for many of these kids will grow up to be our future leaders.

One undisputable way to lead America back to its Christian roots is to take back our schools for Christ. We cannot continue to let the government run the school system and corrupt it, as has been happening. As Christian parents, we need to investigate, find out what is happening and become involved in our children's education, protecting it from every inroad of false teaching. This is an absolute

must. Will you rise to the challenge, beginning today? I
pray that you will.

> Now I sit me down in school
> Where praying is against the rule.
> For this great nation under God
> Finds mention of Him very odd.
>
> If Scriptures say the class recites,
> It violates the Bill of Rights.
> And anytime my head I bow,
> Becomes a federal matter now!
>
> Our hair can be purple, orange or green,
> That's no offense, it's the freedom scene.
> The law is specific, the law is precise,
> Prayers spoken aloud are a serious vice.
>
> For praying in a public hall,
> Might offend those with no faith at all.
> In silence alone we must meditate,
> God's name is prohibited by the State.
>
> We're allowed to cuss and dress like freaks,
> And pierce our nose, our tongue, our cheeks.
> They've outlawed guns; but first the Bible.
> To quote the good Book makes me liable.

We can elect a pregnant Senior queen,
And the unwed daddy, our Senior King.
It's "inappropriate" to teach right from wrong.
We're taught that such "judgments" do not
belong.

We can get our condoms and birth controls,
Study witchcraft, vampires and totem poles.
But the Ten Commandments are not allowed,
No Word of God must reach this crowd.

It's scary here I must confess,
When chaos reigns the school's a mess,
So, Lord, this silent plea I make:
Should I be shot, my soul please take.

—Author unknown

Chapter 12

AN ABSOLUTE MUST!

BLUNTLY STATED, WE need another manifestation of the glory of God to awaken the millions of Americans who are immersed in demonic deception and spiritual blindness that has led to a level of sexual perversion equal to that seen in Sodom and Gomorrah. God had to destroy those cities with fire and brimstone. It is a historical fact the final stage of any civilization in history has been moral decay and complete sexual perversion. That's where America is today. We don't want to have happen to us what happened to those two wicked cities in the Bible. The choice is ours.

Remember the peoples of those two cities did not have the Word of God, nor had they ever heard of the cross. We have, which means we are *"without excuse,"* as we read in Romans 1:20. The majority of Americans have rejected the message of salvation. Does not this in actuality escalate our guilt? If we but realized this, we would realize that this is unbelievably scary and serious.

Please understand this: if we don't immediately work to bring about our desperately needed nationwide awakening, God's wrath will come. It is one or the other. We simply cannot just float along, ignoring the seriousness of the times and be oblivious to the certainty of divine wrath. There must be deep repentance and earnest seeking of God's forgiveness and deliverance in our land. There is only one recourse: as Christians, we must pray together with singleness of heart and soul. It is also of utmost importance that we understand the eternal destiny of the majority of Americans hinges directly on us, God's people, and our praying, our repenting and our standing in the gap (see Ezekiel 22:30-31).

What we so desperately need is a manifestation of our holy God as happened in Korea a century ago. According to Jonathan Goforth, who was there and reported the events in his book *When the Fire Fell*, that divine visitation was total and spread to many nations across the world. Goforth writes there was not even one village in the nation where people were not saved! At the height of that nationwide visitation, it was reported the entire population of some towns were all at church—for the unsaved, now a small minority, had to leave town to escape the divine presence.

Now that is an awakening. And, happily, it was not just an isolated local event. The *entire nation* was literally inundated with God's holy presence (see Isa. 64:1-4). That is what we desperately need now in America—a nationwide, coast-to-coast visitation of our God in all His holiness and glory. And we need it ASAP. When that happens—when countless precious souls meet their Maker and cry out for forgiveness—it will be glorious. Oh, Lord, do it here. Do it now, this year!

I am reminded of the stunning testimonies about powerful manifestations of God's presence during Charles Finney's revivals in America in the early nineteenth century. One report that so moved me was about the times when farmers, totally oblivious as to what was happening, would come to town on personal business and cross an unseen line of divine presence. When they crossed this line, they would fall to the ground, crying out for mercy, and when they arose they were newborn Christians, shouting because of their newfound joy. Now that is an awakening, and that is what our hearts should long for again right here in America.

Let's remember the Day of Pentecost as told in Acts 2. This thrilling account leaves no doubt whatever as to what literally happened. When the 120 were filled with the Holy Spirit, not only were they impacted, but the *entire city* was also inundated with the glorious presence of the Almighty. Thousands came to Christ as a result. Was that just an exception? Definitely not. In fact, this is to be the norm when God comes to town. Hallelujah! Should that not be what we desperately want and need in America today? Happily, it has happened again and again throughout our history. Oh, the awesome stories of God's mighty moving in our three previous awakenings. It can, it must, and it will happen again if we repent, for as we are promised in 2 Chronicles 7:14: "*If my people, which are called by my name [you and I], shall humble themselves, and pray, and seek my face, and turn from their wicked ways; then will I hear from heaven, and will forgive their sin, and will heal their land."*

How I love that last phrase, *"I will heal their land."* God will heal not just one town or city, but *the entire nation*, coast to coast. Does that not give you goose bumps when you think about it? That is God's promise and, without doubt, what He yearns to do. But it cannot and will not happen unless we, His people—you and me included—repent for the nation, pray and keep on asking, persistently, for His mercy to fall on this land. We must literally feel the sins and wickedness of our nation and even be in agony of soul for all the hell-bound people around us and for the nation's vast sinfulness.

This bears repeating, for we need to come to grips with this: *that desperately needed visitation will never come until we, the followers of Christ, fulfill our vital part of the equation.* Bluntly stated, our part is to travail in prayer, repenting for our nation's sins. That's the focus of God's clearly spoken promise in 2 Chronicles 7:14. It is also the central thrust of God's pleas in the book of Joel; namely, that Christians clearly understand the Church's part in this equation is absolutely crucial. We must fulfill our part, or millions will perish eternally.

If we fail to get under this burden to weep and travail in prayer for the sins of our nation—to be so moved by America's awful load of sin that we seek His face—*the awakening will never come.* This is not an easy calling, but it is of utmost importance we understand it could mean that millions will go to glory. Focus on those lost souls. When we get to glory, there will be countless precious souls there because *we travailed* in intercession for them. Dear fellow Christian, a vital part of our calling in Christ is to carry this burden for the lost. And not just a burden for family or friends, but also for the nation. So let's have the attitude of Paul, who penned, *"[I] now rejoice in my sufferings for you, and fill up that which is behind of the afflictions of Christ in my flesh for his body's sake, which is the church"* (Col. 1:24).

Even now with all of our corruption, our God yearns to come down in His glory and sweep even millions into the Kingdom. That's our God! What love! *"The Lord is...not willing that any should perish, but that all come to repentance"* (2 Pet. 3:9). Today, He is calling church congregations to unite in prayer. He is calling individuals as well, but more than that, His call is for congregations to unite as one voice, repenting for the nation. When that occurs, the outpouring of the Holy Spirit will happen. That is when even multiplied millions will be swept into the kingdom.

This is what we long for. This is what we absolutely must have now, even this year—or else. The very future of our Christian republic hinges on it's coming. And, oh, how our God yearns to so move all across our nation. Hear Him: *"Behold ye among the heathen, and regard, and wonder marvelously: for I will work a work in your days which ye will not believe, though it be told you"* (Hab. 1:5). That is God talking...promising...sharing His heart's desire. Later, He says, *"The vision is yet for an appointed time, but at the end it shall speak, and not lie: though it tarry, wait for it; because it will surely come....The earth [nation] shall be filled with the knowledge of the glory of the LORD"* (Hab. 2:3,14). What an awesome promise from the lips of our God!

Christian, you and I together are the key to this great awakening occurring in our nation. It will only come when we, God's people, gather in solemn assemblies to travail for our America. So, will you commit to do this today?

Chapter 13

REVIVALISTS

W ITHOUT A DOUBT, prayer has been the key to any and every awakening throughout history. God's Word is very clear on declaring the utmost importance of prayer. Every outpouring of the Spirit can be traced to God's people being so desperate and hungry for a visitation of the Almighty that they literally gave themselves to it. Nor has it ever been a short, shallow type of praying. No, it has only been when God's people have become so burdened and so passionate that they have given themselves to travail of soul, crying out for a visitation of the Holy Spirit, that the awakenings have come.

The burden of these individuals was for the lost—for a move of God that would sweep countless precious souls into the Kingdom. Many today have also spent hours and days crying out to the Almighty to have mercy on America. Again and again, they have rented out stadiums where God's people could gather by the thousands to pray. I am reminded of the JHOP houses where unceasing prayer is taking place. In the House of Prayer in Kansas, for example, there has been unbroken prayer for more than thirteen years straight. That's awesome! In fact, the list of current prayer gatherings across America is astonishing. There is that much prayer happening 24/7! This is wonderful, and we should rejoice.

However, there is one thing about this whole scenario that has me deeply puzzled. With so much prayer taking place, why are we not yet experiencing revival? Honestly, it seems to me there is more prayer happening across our nation than we have ever had before in our history. Yet there is still no outpouring! What's the explanation? We should all be thankful for the prayers, but why are we not experiencing a visitation of the Lord right now in our land?

There is at least one plausible explanation that has gripped my heart. It might surprise you, but there is no doubt that you will agree. In studying every awakening throughout history (including our own nation's history of revivals), it is evident that God has always raised up powerfully anointed, Spirit-filled vessels to bring about the revival. There appears to be no exception to this rule.

When you read the book of Judges, for example, you can't help but be amazed by the endless account of Israel's never-ending backsliding. Every time Israel forsook the Lord, they fell into the idolatry and evils of the inhabitants of the land. Invariably, sooner or later, they cried out to the Lord in abject repentance. Then what happened—every time? Without exception, the Lord raised up deliverers, anointed human vessels, through whom He brought restoration—a new awakening. For 400 years, there was not one exception. Each time, God's blessing came through powerfully anointed, Spirit-empowered vessels in His hands. Do you see the connection? God always brought deliverance through human instruments. Could this not be the key as to why we're not experiencing the longed-for outpouring of His Spirit here in America? Is this what is missing today and why the revival we need has not yet come?

Continuing, consider John the Baptist, a powerfully Spirit-anointed vessel that rocked Israel. In Matthew we read, *"In those days came John the Baptist, preaching in the wilderness of Judea, and saying, Repent ye: for the kingdom of heaven is at hand.... Then went out to him Jerusalem, and all Judea, and all the region round about Jordan, and were baptized of him in Jordan"* (3:1-2,5-6). This passage clearly states the nation flocked to hear John and countless numbers of people confessed their sins and were baptized. Clearly, John was a mightily anointed revivalist, and through him the nationwide awakening came.

In the history of revivals here in America (and in every other outpouring a well), when deeply concerned followers of Christ gave themselves to unceasing prayer and brokenheartedly repented for their nation's wickedness, the Lord *always* raised up revivalists who were so empowered by the Holy Spirit that people everywhere repented and came back to God in great numbers. Oh, the crowds that flocked to hear them. At times the numbers were so large they had to go outdoors. It is said that George Whitfield often preached without a microphone to crowds of 20,000 and more. Multitudes came to Christ, and America was once again transformed spiritually.

When you think about the revivals we have had in America, the names of many mightily anointed revivalists come to mind: Jonathan Edwards, John Wesley and David Brainerd in the eighteenth century; Charles Finney, Charles Spurgeon, Dwight Moody, Billy Sunday and many more in the nineteenth century. Without ceasing, millions of sinners were constantly led to the Savior during these revivals.

Many of us have our own wonderful memories of those awesome days during the twentieth century when the Lord raised up William Seymour of the Azusa Street outpouring. Then there were Charles Price, Amy McPherson, David du Plessis and Oral Roberts, to name but a few. And what about the wonderful Billy Graham Crusades held in huge stadiums filled to capacity? Many of us will never forget the awesome sight of seeing thousands of people streaming to the front to receive Christ. It was happening all the time, all across the nation. Glory!

But, as of right now, no mightily anointed revivalists are moving across America and holding revivals in tents, or in stadiums, or anywhere else for that matter? There are no revivalists out there pointing great numbers of precious lost souls to Christ in the way that we used to hear. Think about when you last heard about or attended such an event. Probably not in recent years. This is a sad fact and a matter of extreme concern, and we should be earnestly praying to see these taking place again. But are we? Honestly, I am not hearing such. And so, today in America, as in the days of Israel centuries ago, the masses are engulfed in utter corruption—so much so that God has "*given them up to uncleanness through the lusts of their own hearts"* (Rom. 1:24). What a terrifying portrayal of where we are in America today.

Thankfully, as Israel did centuries ago, many of us are on our faces repenting brokenheartedly, asking the Lord to forgive and deliver our nation. But we need to make a definite shift in our prayer emphasis. Instead of praying for *ourselves,* Christ's followers, we need to focus on the lost all around us, and we also need to be crying out for the Lord to raise up anointed revivalists. We need several revivalists to crisscross the nation, lifting up the name of Jesus and leading great numbers to the Lord. Oh, for another glorious day when we see long lines of sinners at the altars receiving Christ!

So we see that when God brings revival to this land, He will do it in the same way as He has done throughout history: by raising powerfully anointed preachers to call the nation to repentance and restoration. The cry that rises in our hearts should be for a new day when we will hear and see countless sinners coming to Christ again. It should be for men and women to rise up today who are as mightily anointed as were George Whitfield, Jonathan Edwards and Charles Finney in their day. Oh, for the Lord to raise up ten—better still, twenty—John the Baptists this year here in America! We are more than 300 million strong, so we need a mighty band of revivalists to reach everyone with the good news of Christ.

Chapter 14

CHRISTIAN AMERICA?

N OT ANY MORE! It's absolutely sickening to have to admit this, but we can no longer be called a Christian nation, as less than twenty percent of Americans are followers of Christ—and we are told that only six percent of today's churchgoing members have a true biblical worldview. How disturbing! It's no wonder we've lost our power to witness and win souls right here in our homeland. I find this statistic extremely disconcerting, and my heart weeps as I face this issue in honesty.

As previously mentioned, we can no longer be considered a Christian nation when estimates state that there are only sixty million Christians. Because the population in our country is more than 300 million, this means that there is *one* follower of Christ for every *five* Americans. Many people were sickened and even angered when they heard President Obama declare in a speech that America is a post-Christian people. Many felt deep pain when they heard this, for most of us have honestly believed that we still are a Christian country. But not so. If only we realized it.

It's time, fellow Christians, for us to get serious about this. The statistics support President Obama's statement. *And if that doesn't arouse us to action, then we are in deep trouble spiritually.* If we are true followers of the Lord Jesus, it will move us to action. Sure, we have sent thousands of missionaries around the world to win souls, but what about here in our homeland? As a Church, we've failed miserably. While we were winning souls in nations around the world, we have allowed millions here to be deceived and reject God's Word and our Lord Jesus. How tragic that today the majority of our fellow Americans are hell-bound. It hurts me so deeply to have to admit it. Oh, God, help us to turn this around, beginning this year.

How can we be considered a Christian nation when we can't pray in Jesus' name, read our Bibles or witness for Christ on school campuses or at public gatherings in Washington D.C.? Or when creation is not allowed to be taught and evolution is proclaimed as the truth in all our schools? Or when the majority of our people never darken a church door and vast numbers of our population are enmeshed in the lies of cults that thrive everywhere? Or when many church doors are closing and pastors' wives are imploring their husbands to give up pastoring? Or when the porno industry has engulfed a high percentage of our nation's pastors? Or when evangelism is at an all-time low—and when we do evangelize, we are mocked and even threatened? Or when most Christians don't take a stand to defend their faith or stop the vile practice of murdering our babies?

How can we be considered a Christian nation when our school system caters to the Muslim community, giving them the freedom to observe their faith in our schools while Christians are not? I saw with my own eyes on television that large crowd of Muslims on their knees worshiping Allah on the streets of New York. As I mentioned, they were blocking traffic, and the authorities allowed it. Why? Because we Christians are allowing it...by saying and doing nothing. We don't even demand that our children be allowed to pray, say the Lord's Prayer, and read their Bibles on campus. We simply cave in, thereby allowing those of various non-Christian faiths to come in and take over.

Sadly, the reasons for why we are no longer a Christian nation are endless, so I will not continue to enumerate such heartbreaking facts. However, because all of this is true, it means that more than 240 million Americans today are not followers of our precious Lord Jesus. They are lost—hell-bound. What this means is that our homeland—America—has become a mission field. If that doesn't move us, what will? And, believe it or not, the Lord is sending missionaries to our country to win the lost in America to Christ. These missionaries are coming from Africa, Asia, and many places where America used to send missionaries. How the tables have turned. It's truly wonderful that God is sending them here, but should it also not convict and powerfully move us Christians to new levels of action?

In response to these tragic facts, we, the Church, need to deeply repent and take purposeful action. We need to become instruments in the Holy Spirit's hands that are so anointed that millions turn to a vibrant faith in Jesus Christ.

We need to do this at any cost—fearlessly, courageously, and everywhere proclaiming God's Word. Oh, for the day when we again see lost souls thronging to our altars for salvation.

Our goal—dare we say it—must be to restore America back to its Christian roots and stomp out the corruption that abounds in our government at all levels. We must wrench our education system out of the hands of government and once again be involved in every decision and every course that is taught to our children. It's imperative we think big—for God is on our side. So let's be fully committed to taking America back, for we can, we will, and we must. Our founding fathers fought a world power and won at great cost. Some of them lost their lives, and others lost their fortunes. Today it is our turn. Dare we do any less for our posterity?

Give up? Never! Let's repent first and then arise, totally assured that we will win. It won't be easy but, as I have said, it can be done—not in our strength, but in the Lord's: *"'Not by might nor by power, but by my Spirit,' says the LORD"* (Zech. 4:6, NIV). Let's never forget this is a war against both a seen and an unseen enemy. As Paul exhorts in his letter to the Ephesians, *"I want to remind you that your strength must come from the Lord's mighty power within you. Put on all of God's armor so that you will be able to stand safe against all strategies and tricks of Satan. For we are not fighting against people made of flesh and blood, but against persons without bodies—the evil rulers of the unseen world, those mighty satanic beings and great evil princes of darkness who rule this world; and against huge numbers of wicked spirits in the spirit world. So use every piece of God's armor....Pray all the time.*

Ask God for anything in line with the Holy Spirit's wishes. Plead with him, reminding him of your needs and keep praying earnestly" (Eph. 6:10–13, 18 TLB).

Let's be encouraged and inspired by those in the Early Church who were so effective in their witness for Christ that ultimately the vast Roman Empire accepted Christianity as its state religion. There is no doubt we will be able to win our America back to serving our Lord. Hallelujah! Yes, we can do it...and we must.

Chapter 15

ONLY IMAGINE

WHAT LIES BEFORE us here in what used to be Christian America? Let's take note of the challenges that are happening to our cherished freedoms today and, with the Lord's help, grasp what our beloved America will soon be like if we continue down the path we're walking today. It is of utmost importance that we see what is now taking place right before our eyes—the path that our liberal leaders are leading us down. If nothing is done to change our course, we will soon see the following:

- *No more Bibles allowed,* because God's Word is classified as the "hate book." Why? Because the Bible clearly condemns as wrong and evil many current lifestyles and practices that today are common and accepted.

- *No more worship services* where God's Word is powerfully proclaimed, or where we sing those glorious old hymns and songs about the blood, the cross, and heaven—the joys of salvation.

- *No more witnessing* to the lost to lead men and women to Christ. No speaking about sin, divine wrath, judgment or hell.

- *No more public proclamation that Jesus saves and that He alone* is the way, the truth, and the life. Our Christian faith will be a thing of the past, and ultimately a new religion (such as Islam) will be forced upon us, or no faith at all (as in Europe, which is today only one percent Christian).

- *No more home gatherings for Bible studies,* for if we do, some authorities will come and break it up and possibly arrest the leaders.

- *No more evangelistic crusades* where the good news is preached and sinners are free to come to the altars to receive Jesus Christ as their Savior.

- *No more public displays of Christian truths in any form* on billboards, our clothes or anywhere else about the truths of God's Word or about the forgiveness of sins and the need to receive Jesus as Savior.

- *No more proclamation of the gospel on the airwaves, and no more conservative talk show hosts.* All will be gone. All we will be left with is state-controlled endless propaganda and liberal garbage.

- *No more freedom to bow our heads publicly* to pray and give thanks for our food.

- *No more Christian schools or home schooling,* as children will be educated by the state.

- *No more Christian books*—even our Bibles—*on the market*, as all will be confiscated and destroyed.
- *No more freedom to choose our careers*—all people will be tested and told by the government where they will work and serve.
- *No more private enterprises.* Instead, everyone will serve the state. Personal initiative will die.
- *No more freedom, period.* Ultimately, we will all become the property of the state.

Of course, this will not happen immediately, because our newly appointed big-government leaders know full well there would be massive uprisings to fight and oppose it. Sadly they are achieving their goals, seemingly with little resistance. We've always been a people of faith in God's Word, but sadly, we're rapidly losing out to the liberal element in our society. It takes time, but if the current government leaders have their way, they will win. If we who love Christ want to maintain our Christian roots, every one of us must speak up and take a stand.

At first, as I have said, there will be many uprisings as the lovers of our cherished freedoms unite to resist—to fight—to keep our freedoms. We must pray there will not be bloodshed, if at all possible, with our Lord's help. Let's not forget recent history. When communism (and, if truth be told, we are headed that way) took over in Russia, an estimated seventy million people died. In China under Mao's corrupt regime, thirty million lost their lives. And let's not forget what happened in Germany when socialism took over. Sheer horror and tragedy. It grieves me and scares me to be writing this, and in no way do any of us want it. We want our freedoms and, if possible, we want them without bloodshed. However, in remembering our own history, we know that many paid dearly to win our cherished freedoms. Understand this, freedom does not come easily.

If you are still thinking, *This is America and it will never happen here,* you need to understand it has already begun to happen. Our President has surrounded himself with leaders of extremely questionable backgrounds, not one of whom is a Christian. What's more, he has illegally appointed more than thirty czars to run the banks and businesses he has taken over, and they report only to him, not Congress. Is this not already a dictatorship, at least to a disconcerting degree?

Imagine what all this means to us freedom-loving, Bible-believing Americans. We must open our eyes and see it. Hopefully, it's not too late. Those of us who love our free country and our biblical roots can still wake up, mobilize, unite, and take action. No, I am not suggesting we take up guns to shoot and kill. (By the way, our leaders intend to take those freedoms away as well and make it illegal to own guns.) But we need to remember that when our founding fathers fought for their faith, they used guns, and many died. Oh, that this might not have to happen again in our day.

We can thank God we regained control of the House in the 2010 election, and won seven new seats in the Senate. But while we are rejoicing, it's imperative we understand this is but the beginning of a long uphill battle to win America back to its Christian heritage. That has to be our goal, and nothing short of that—agreed? Oh, how every intercessor and every concerned Christian must unceasingly pray for our newly elected leaders. And understand this: when these newcomers go to Washington D.C., they will run headlong into much evil, including bribery and countless subtle temptations. Our capital is inundated in such. We can also be sure that our unseen enemy will work overtime to win them to his cause. In the past, all too often, our newly elected leaders have succumbed to the horrendous pressures of Washington. But not this time—if we stand united with them in unceasing prayer and take action.

I strongly suggest that you, intercessor and concerned fellow Christian, make a list of our leaders (especially those who are followers of Christ) and commit to (1) praying daily for them, and (2) communicating with them as the Lord leads you to encourage them. In short, let's be a vital part of what is happening in our nation's capital and not get so involved in living that we forget them. For is it not true that in the past most of us have seldom, if ever, done this? Well, now is the time! And as we do our part, Almighty God will move both in our capital and across our beloved America.

Chapter 16

THE NAME ABOVE
ALL NAMES: JESUS!

L ET US LOOK at one final catastrophic situation that has been perpetrated on our beloved land. Please prayerfully think about this: today, the name of our precious Jesus, who is King of kings, Lord of lords, and both the Creator and sustainer of the universe, is publicly and unabashedly being mocked. If someone in Washington, D.C., or at a school graduation mentions His name, the anti-Christ godless unite with one angry voice, crying out against it! How sad! How tragic!

Only a few decades ago this would not have happened, as there would have been an outcry by millions of His followers in protest. But today we hear almost not even a peep. Why? How is this possible? This mocking of our faith escalates unceasingly. Where will it end? Will we—you, I and fellow Christians everywhere—continue to be silent and afraid to speak up for our glorious Lord Jesus and His cause?

If anyone says or publishes anything negative—even something factual—about Islam, the whole Muslim world rises up in burning anger and even seeks to kill the person who dared to speak. We've seen it again and again. Remember the pastor in Florida who planned to burn the Quran? Islamic nations rose up in outrage. The net result? Silence and fearfulness to say anything negative about Islam.

How is it that the followers of Jesus Christ, who alone is the Savior of all mankind, don't speak up for their Lord? Are we ashamed of Him? Could it be that we fear being ridiculed or mocked? It certainly seems so. Our Lord clearly commands, *"Ye are the light of the world....Let your light so shine before men"* (Matt. 5:14, 16). When we are silent, we are definitely not letting our light shine. Jesus also says, *"Whosoever shall be ashamed of me and of my words, of him shall the Son of man be ashamed, when he shall come in his own glory, and in his Father's, and of the holy angels"* (Luke 9:26).

Back in the days of the Early Church, the believers openly proclaimed idols and heathen religions to be false and Jesus alone to be the Savior of the world. No one knows how many Christians were martyred, let alone persecuted, for proclaiming that name which is above every name: Jesus. Right here in our beloved homeland, until recently, faithful followers of Christ have boldly proclaimed His name. His name was revered and mentioned with passion and power.

But today, His name cannot even be mentioned in public places. Where has our freedom of speech gone? That has always been one of our most prized freedoms, but such is not the case today. However, those in other camps—atheists, evolutionists, liberals, proclaimers of other religions—openly speak about what they believe and seek to propagate it. Atheists are especially bold. But not the followers of Jesus Christ. The reigning word in our society today is *tolerance*. We are told that we must not ever say that there is no salvation apart from the Lord Jesus. That is offensive. This results in a watered-downed gospel and the masses not understanding the truth. Again, is this not one reason that the majority of our fellow Americans are nonbelievers?

Tolerance is precisely what the enemy wants, because little by little that liberal element has chipped away our religious freedom until we've almost lost it. And we probably will lose it soon—unless we take action. It's imperative we understand the enemy's goal is to totally shut us up and keep us from witnessing. When this happens, countless more souls go to a Christless eternity.

Today, we need champions to mobilize Christians across the United States to become one mighty voice committed to winning our freedom back. Let's not just leave it up to someone else to take the lead. Let's all rise to the challenge, empowered by the Holy Spirit. Oh, for Christian congressmen, senators, and others in key positions to have the courage to mention in public—anywhere and everywhere—the name of Jesus Christ and to pray in His name. Let's communicate words of inspiration and encouragement to them. Let's pray they be so empowered by the Holy Spirit they will boldly lift up not only Jesus' name but also be God's vital instruments to restore our nation to our Christian roots.

Remember this nation was founded on God's Word. It is of utmost importance that we purpose in our hearts as followers of Christ to be vital instruments in His hands so that He can make this a Christian nation once again. We must desperately desire to keep America truly Christian and restore it to its former faith and witness. Every true follower of our Lord Jesus, old and young, must be involved and committed to this goal. How? By praying and mobilizing in prayer, by writing letters, and by letting the Lord use us much more. Each of us are essential in this battle to restore America to its Christian roots. Each one of us. Rejoice and get excited. All God needs is yielded and obedient followers. It will be through His giftings in us that the victory will be won. He will give each of us new gifts so we might be used more. Never ask, "Can God do it?" Rather, cry out, "God can—even through me!"

Why do we have to cater to these other religious faiths when we know we are followers of Christ? It's totally wrong and completely unnecessary for us to yield to the demands of atheists, evolutionists, and others who want us to shut up and hide our witness. That's what the enemy wants, and so far he has been winning. He wants us to surrender to these groups so we will backslide and our witness will shut down. That is precisely his goal. But no longer. We will not submit to the demands of these groups.

We must unite and get bolder in lifting up the name of Jesus even in the face of ridicule, cursing, threats or more. Of course, this doesn't mean we will be unkind or force those of other faiths, including atheists, to become Christians. However, we have to tell them the truth—that Jesus alone is the way, the truth, and the life—whether they like it or not. Because we know they are lost, we have to lift up the name of our Lord Jesus, who alone is the Savior of the world. *"For there is none other name under heaven given among men, whereby we must be saved"* (Acts 4:12). We dare not be silent, for our God clearly says, *"If thou dost not speak to warn the wicked from his way, that wicked man will die in his iniquity; but his blood will I require at thine hand"* (Ezek. 33:8).

We must never allow the influences of other religions or the demands of atheists to shut down our witness, even if it means persecution, prison or worse. It probably will, sooner or later. Let's never forget that throughout history, millions of Christians have suffered immeasurably and have died for lifting up the name of Christ and refusing to keep quiet. Even today around the world, fellow Christians are suffering for their witness. But do they shut up? Never! So why should we in America shut down our witness simply because those who hate our Jesus demand that we not tell them the truth?

I repeat: our calling is to talk about Jesus and let everyone know that without Him they are lost and hell-bound. It is to be expected that many will hate us, and the day is coming when we will be arrested for lifting up that name. Our Lord clearly states, *"The time cometh, that whosoever killeth you will think that he doeth God service. And these things will they do unto you, because they have not known the Father, nor me. But these things have I told you, that when the time shall come, ye may remember that I told you of them"* (John 16:2-4). Persecution is to be expected, but it is never a reason for stopping our witness. Throughout history, the

Church has always been at its strongest when it has had to endure suffering.

Christians one and all, wake up, pray up, speak up, and stand up for Christ and our faith, regardless of the cost. It is imperative we remember the Word clearly says, *"For unto you it is given in the behalf of Christ, not only to believe on him, but also to suffer for His sake"* (Phil 1:29). In 1 Peter 4:12-14, we also read, *"Beloved, think it not strange concerning the fiery trial which is to try you, as though some strange thing happened unto you: But rejoice, inasmuch as ye are partakers of Christ's sufferings; that, when His glory shall be revealed, ye may be glad also with exceeding joy. If ye be reproached for the name of Christ, happy are ye; for the Spirit of glory and of God resteth upon you: on their part he is evil spoken of, but on your part he is glorified."*

Beginning today, let's stop this spirit of compromise. Let's quit capitulating to Satan's schemes to destroy our Christian roots and make America a godless, atheistic or Islamic nation. Let's bind that vile enemy who wants to shut the mouth of every follower of Jesus Christ here in America. Although he is winning right now, Christians can reverse this trend by no longer being silent and afraid to be shining witnesses for Christ, especially in public places. So let's pray for a mighty move of the Holy Spirit in Christians' hearts across this nation that once again Jesus' name shall be on the lips of His people everywhere with power, boldness, and unlimited freedom.

Always remember these words from Philippians: *"Wherefore God also hath highly exalted him, and given him a name which is above every name: That at the name of*

Jesus every knee should bow, of things in heaven, and things in earth, and things under the earth; and that every tongue should confess that Jesus Christ is Lord, to the glory of God the Father" (2:9–11). The day will come when every person shall confess that Jesus is the eternal Son of God and the only Savior of all mankind. Oh, for that day to happen in our lifetime!

Chapter 17

A PRAYER FOR AMERICA

O, *LORD, LIKE Daniel of old, we come to You confessing the unbridled wickedness of our great nation—a nation that was founded so we might serve the Lord Jesus Christ, the Lord of the universe. Thank You for the faith of our founding fathers. Oh, how You blessed us like no other nation on earth when as a people we honored You.*

But today, dear Lord, there are many among us—and among our leaders—who are committed to wiping out every vestige of faith in Jesus Christ. Our greatest enemies are from within. We have trained them in our schools, and now we are reaping the evils. The spirit of antichrist has swept in and is rapidly taking away our cherished freedoms in Christ that many of our forefathers died to obtain. These enemies are committed to removing the freedom to proclaim Christ publicly. Their sole objective is to make our once-Christian America into an atheistic, anti-Christ nation. All other false gods are permitted, but not the name of Jesus who alone is Lord of lords and King of kings, and the one at whose knee every person of all the ages shall one day bow. Oh, God, it is this name that is above every name that they hate, which is why they hate us who love Him and live to serve Him. God, help us! Hear our cries! In deepest sorrow of heart, we repent and earnestly ask and plead for Your forgiveness and help.

In many areas of government today, the glorious name of Jesus must not be said publicly, for fear there will be outcries of opposition. Forgive us for allowing this to happen. It has occurred because we, Your followers, did not speak up. Sadly, we chose to shut up, submitting to these groups because of fear and intimidation. Now we are reaping what we have sowed!

In our schools, our children are not permitted to bow their heads in prayer. The Bible is out, for it is considered to be a book of hate. Why? Because Your Word condemns as sin countless evil practices that are not only common in our nation but are also accepted and proclaimed as being normal and right. Oh, how far we have fallen from being a godly people! Groups opposed to the gospel have even succeeded in having the Ten Commandments removed from public display. Why? Because, as one of our Supreme Court judges declared, "They will influence us to obey them." In other words, people in our nation want the freedom to live a lifestyle contrary to Your specific commands, Oh Lord Almighty! What a terrible commentary on the true state of affairs in our country today!

Our Father in heaven, hear our cries! We implore You to remove from leadership every person who is leading us into apostasy. Cause these leaders to be rejected and not re-elected. Oh, God, we pray earnestly that men and women who love and revere Your name, like our godly forefathers, will be elected.

Your Word declares that You put men in authority, so please cause the wicked to be removed. We want only those who honor and love You to be in power. Hear our cry!

God, the list of our national sins is endless. They exceed those of Sodom and Gomorrah, who did not have the light as we have had it—and You destroyed them with fire and brimstone. Oh, Lord, we truly do not deserve Your forgiveness! Our national cup of iniquity is overflowing. It is only because of Your mercies that we have not already been consumed.

There is no doubt whatsoever that You have not poured out Your wrath because in our midst are countless deeply concerned intercessors who unceasingly are pleading for You to forgive our sins and heal our land. Our united plea is that in Your mercy, You will grant another window of time for national repentance, instead of Your wrath. We are crying out for another nationwide visitation of Your glorious presence that will sweep millions into Your kingdom.

God, we thank You for every travailing intercessor who sees the horrible clouds of looming judgment but who also knows that You are a forgiving and merciful God. We recall, too, that it was 100 years ago during the Azusa Street outpouring that You promised there would be an even greater outpouring in our day. So now—even this year—we implore You grant us that promised visitation. With broken and contrite hearts, we confess we do not deserve it. Yet we know You are a merciful God who has deferred pouring out His wrath because You are not willing that any should perish, but all should come to the knowledge of the truth. Your heart is to forgive. Hallelujah! You long for multitudes to repent and be swept into Your kingdom. Oh, that it might come now—this year!

We are standing firmly on Your awesome promise in 2 Chronicles 7:14, which says, "If my people, who are called by my name, will humble themselves and pray and will seek my face and turn from their wicked ways, then I will hear from heaven, and I will forgive their sin and will heal their land."

Today, and every day, we are calling on Your name. We humble ourselves and with broken hearts confess our sins—the multitude of sins of our nation. We repent! Oh, how as a nation we have sinned and blasphemed Your name. We have caused countless millions worldwide to sin as well through our corrupting pornography that we have transmitted over the world's airwaves. Lord, we cry out in abject anguish of heart because of our nation's evils. We turn to You, asking for mercy and that the glorious visitation of Your presence would come down among us. For when this happens, there will be true repentance and a turning from our sins. Oh, happy day! Multitudes wondrously experiencing Your mercy and the unlimited joys of Your salvation!

This is Your promise that we see vividly portrayed in the book of Joel. In obedience to Your pleas, we turn to You with all our hearts, with fasting and with weeping, and cry unceasingly, "Spare thy people, O LORD, and give not thine heritage to reproach, that the heathen should rule over them: wherefore should they say among the people, Where is their God?" (Joel 2:17). Your glorious promise is, "It shall come to pass afterward, that I will pour out my Spirit upon all" (v. 28). We claim it! We rejoice in it! Right here in our beloved homeland, with eager expectation, we are looking for our fourth visitation!

Isaiah's passionate heart cry of centuries long ago is our heart cry today: "Oh, that thou wouldest rend the heavens, that thou wouldest come down, that the mountains might flow down at they presence...to make they name known to thine adversaries, that the nations may tremble at Your presence! When thou didst terrible things which we looked not for, thou camest down, the mountains flowed down at they presence. For since the beginning of the world men have not heard...neither hath the eye seen, O God, beside thee, what he hath prepared for him that waiteth for him" (Isa. 64:1–4). O, Lord, this is what we yearn for with unlimited eager anticipation. Glory! It's Your heart! It's Your promise!

We are watchmen on the walls who will never hold our peace day or night. We who make mention of the Your name will not keep silent, and we will not rest until You establish and make the Church a praise in the earth. Hallelujah, I am one of them! Thank You, Lord, for this privilege and honor!

Chapter 18

LAST CHANCE,

AMERICA?

THIS QUESTION BURNS in my heart, crying out for an answer—the *right* answer. Oh, Church of Jesus Christ, don't you see the handwriting on the wall? All the indications right here in our beloved and once-strong Christian nation scream, "See it! The time is now—or God's wrath!" That's a fact.

Understand that we are so very guilty. No people have had more light than us. Our founding fathers were godly, Bible believing men of God. How God blessed us and made us a blessing to countless millions around the world—many of whom came to be one of us. For decades we've sent missionaries to the far corners of the earth and, as of right now, we still are. Praise God!

But something drastic—no, better said, something terrifying—has happened and *is* happening right before our very eyes. Yet, tragically, most of us do not see it or, even worse, we know it but *do nothing to turn it around!* To put it bluntly, evil is triumphing on almost every front, and we are not mobilizing to take action. We are not taking God's call-for-action and uniting in prayer, *with entire congregations crying out to God!*

Thank God that some among us are heartbroken and many precious intercessors are praying. Hallelujah! But as a Church—His body—we're not falling on our faces and *repenting and weeping for our nation.* How is it possible that so many of God's people continue on in their lives without going to their knees and weeping in total repentance? Why is it that most of us are not consumed with a holy fear that drives us to our knees, praying and pleading for the visitation we so desperately need? Please understand I am not criticizing. I am deeply concerned and puzzled about it.

Church, let's go to our knees! Let's unite and hear our God's pleas. Better yet, let's hear His clearly spelled-out command to call solemn assemblies to fast, weep, repent and plead for a turnaround *now* in our once-but-no-more-godly nation. The need is urgent—it's *desperate!* It's now or never. God's imminent wrath is upon us. The time is, oh, so urgent.

And hear this too: the eternal destiny of millions of precious souls hinges on our prayers—right here in our beloved America. That's a fact. This could be our *last chance as a nation.* Understand this as well: If and when we do repent and turn back to God, He will answer and will open the windows of heaven. He will pour out His Spirit in revival blessing. Then, and only then, will our unbelievably wicked America be delivered. There's only one path, beloved, that we can take for this to occur. Has the urgency gripped your heart? *It must.* All of us—every

Christian right now in judgment-bound America—need to respond. We all truly need to come to grips with the reality of our situation. May it grab us to the point that it brings an immediate and passionate response of obedience on our part. We need this desperately! Earnestly! Unceasingly!

We need not go into detail about the endless evils of our nation. We are all painfully aware of them. In Romans 1, Paul clearly spells out America's true wicked condition. Now that's extremely scary and serious. Added to this is the stunning number of churches nationwide that have backslidden and are allowing themselves to be *united with Islam*. It is called "Chrislam," and it is happening in the Church of Jesus Christ, believe it or not. Sickening? Yes! Unthinkable? Yes! Talk about our enemy triumphing. He is, big time! Let us weep and travail for God to open eyes and hearts to the tragedy this is. God, help us. Awaken us.

This is appalling, for we know that practitioners of Islam follow and worship Lucifer, who is Allah. He was cast out of glory for seeking to usurp the throne of Almighty God. Today, the vast majority of Earth's inhabitants worship and follow his cruel dictates. Even here, in what was once Christian America, the enemy is successfully deceiving weak and spiritually shallow Christians in churches across the United States to align with his side. Stunning! Heartbreaking! Tragic! If we could grasp it, we would be appalled at the true spiritual state of our beloved homeland today. Oh, God, somehow open our eyes to see what You see.

When we observe this happening in our Christian America, we need to wake up and cry out to our Almighty Lord for mercy and revival—the only thing that will turn this situation around. We desperately need a Fourth Awakening right now…this year…this minute…today!

My heart is so heavily burdened, dear fellow Christian, and yours is probably burdened as well. *I truly fear that this is our last chance.* We can either obey God now, or our holy heavenly Father will have to pour out His fierce wrath on our land. Our God is loving, and He longs passionately to forgive and sweep into His kingdom as many of those deceived and lost souls as He possibly can. Hallelujah! That is His heart. *But it will not happen without our—yours and mine—participation and obedience.* We absolutely have to fulfill our part, as we see so clearly portrayed in Joel and in many other Scriptures. The Church must grasp the absolute necessity and awesome privilege we have of partnering with the Almighty Himself in winning America back to the truth and our Lord Jesus Christ! Get excited! Let's do it!

Again, to put it plainly, our essential part in this is to go to our knees in unceasing, united prayer and repent for the millions in our nation. We must soak in the prophecies of Joel and hear our Lord's pleas—both His commands *and* His promises. When we do, we can be assured that He will pour out His Spirit on all flesh. The nation will rock in His presence and glory. Countless millions will find Christ. Our youth will be filled with the Spirit and delivered from Satan's grip. Hear this again: *If we don't do this, God's wrath will be poured out*, and the awakening that so many of us long for will never happen. Is that clear? Lord, help us, quicken us.

Let these words deeply sink into your heart: God longs for the awakening to come, but it will not happen until the

Church—His people—come to grips with the true situation and go to their knees in unceasing, travailing prayer and deepest repentance. Then and only then will His longed-for promise in Habakkuk 1:5 and 2:14 be fulfilled: *"Look among the nations and watch—be utterly astounded! For I will work a work in your days which you would not believe, though it were told you.... For the earth will be filled with the knowledge of the glory of the LORD, as the waters cover the sea."*

VOTING,

AN IMPORTANT DUTY

COULD IT EVER be God's first choice to raise up a leader of our nation who is contrary to the Bible's standards? Could it be His choice to raise up someone who detests the Bible and calls it a hate book, even seeking to make it illegal to mention the name of Jesus, the Savior of the world, publicly? Definitely not!

Do you truthfully believe it would be God's will for a Christian nation to be led by such a person? Oh, we need to think this through. When such a leader is elected, we often hear Christians say, "God put him there!" But it would be more accurate to say God *allowed* that person to be elected because of our failure as Christ's followers to vote in unity for a godly leader.

Of course, it is God who *"changes times and seasons; he sets up kings and deposes them"* (Dan. 2:21, NIV). We all agree *"that the Most High ruleth in the kingdom of men, and giveth it to whomsoever he will"* (Dan. 4:25). Things here on earth—in America—do go amuck! Some leaders are corrupt and lead us far from the standards of God's Word. This is what is happening today under the current administration—an administration that can only be seen as corrupt and contrary to God's Word. If the truth were told, this administration gives evidence of a deliberate plan to wipe out every trace of our Christian roots. Millions of people are deeply concerned—probably even terrified! They can see the handwriting on the wall. Thankfully, many are rising to speak out and even resist. Thank God.

This raises a question that demands an answer: how did this happen? Factually stated, these liberals won by default. Is this not true when statistics show that only half of Christians in America are registered to vote and that only half of those who are registered even bother voting? That's sickening, is it not? Every follower of Christ needs to understand the liberals who hate Christian America vote with one voice. They are united. Therefore, it is absolutely imperative that if we truly want to keep God-fearing men and women in leadership, we also need to vote only for those who are true followers of Jesus Christ. It is vital for us to realize that Christians who do not vote are actually voting for liberals. If only they really grasped this fact.

We must understand that God would give us godly leaders like George Washington if we united with one voice in prayer and in our voting. Our God is merciful, and He yearns to bless us and sweep millions back into His kingdom, but we, His people, must faithfully do our part. We must pray, and we must vote. It's of utmost importance that every follower of Christ fully realize voting is both a privilege and a duty.

Renowned historian David Barton wrote, "The Founders understood this, and one of the most frequently quoted Bible principles invoked by the Founders is Proverbs 29:2: "When the righteous rule, the people rejoice; when the wicked rule, the people groan." The key to good government is not how good our documents are or how good our laws are; rather, it is how good our leaders are. In America, whether the righteous rule, or whether the wicked rule depends totally upon the will of the voters: we have our choice."[1]

President Garfield was a minister of the gospel. A century ago he said, "Now more than ever the people are responsible for the character of their Congress. If that body be ignorant, reckless, and corrupt, it is because the people tolerate ignorance, recklessness, and corruption. If it be intelligent, brave, and pure, it is because the people demand these high qualities to represent them in the national legislature....If the next centennial does not find us a great nation...it will be because those who represent the enterprise, the culture, and the morality of the nation do not aid in controlling the political forces."[2]

Charles Finney, a revivalist during the nineteenth century, wrote, "The church must take right ground in regard to politics....The time has come that Christians must vote for honest men, and take consistent ground in politics.... Christians have been exceedingly guilty in this matter. But the time has come when they must act differently....God cannot sustain this free and blessed country, which we love and pray for, unless the church will take right ground....It seems sometimes as if the foundations of the nation were becoming rotten: and Christians seem to act is if they think

God did not see what they do in politics. But I tell you, he does see it; and he will bless or curse this nation according to the course they take."[3]

In conclusion, we need to understand that if God truly had His way: in the elections, through our very instrumentality—namely, by every Christian voting—godly men and women would be elected. There is no way it would be otherwise. Think about it this way: God's real choice would never be to have a person elected whose goal was to wipe out our Christian faith and our worldwide influence for Christ.

So, Church, let's earnestly pray that every precious fellow Christian nationwide will fully come to understand the great importance and necessity of their voting—and to prayerfully vote only for godly men and women to lead us. Let's also pray that God will raise godly men and women of vision and courage in the nation's next elections. As this happens, the heralds of the glorious good news will continue to flow from America's shores to lost souls around the world. Our witness for Christ will continue. Oh, for the next awakening to come soon…hopefully this year!

ENDNOTES

1. David Barton, "The Role of Pastors and Christians," part 11, March 5, 2009. http://www.davidbarton. net/2010/03/05/the-role-of-pastors-and-christians-part-eleventh-by-david-barton/.
2. James A. Garfield, quoted in Burke Hinsdale, editor, *The Works of James Abram Garfield* (Boston: James R. Osgood and Company, 1883), vol. 2, pp. 486,489.
3. Charles G. Finney, *Lectures on Revivals of Religion* (New York: Leavitt, Lord & Co., 1835).

CPSIA information can be obtained at www.ICGtesting.com
Printed in the USA
LVOW13s0858210813

348845LV00001B/79/P